GET YOUR BOOK WRITTEN

Jacquelyn Elnor Johnson

Crimson Hill
Books

www.crimsonhillbooks.com

First print edition, June 2017.

Canadian Cataloguing in Publication Data

Jacquelyn Elnor Johnson

Get Your Book Written

Print edition: ISBN 978-1-988650-27-2

Electronic book edition: ISBN 978-1-988650-26-5

1. Book Ghostwriting 2. Career development 3. Book writing 4. Leadership 5. Influence 6. Thought leaders I. Title II. Author

Cover design: Jacquelyn Elnor Johnson
Cover Image: Faberr Ink/Shutterstock.com
Book design: Jesse Johnson

Crimson Hill Books

(a division of)

Crimson Hill Products Inc.

Wolfville, Nova Scotia

CANADA

Contents

Foreword

When Jackie Johnson asked me to write the foreword to her new book **Get Your Book Written,** I was both surprised and delighted. This is the second time I'd be involved with Jackie producing a book.

Several years ago, she and I sat in my backyard enjoying a glass of wine and discussing what else we would like to do beyond our current jobs. I mentioned that it would be interesting to put together a directory of professional women in the Waterloo Region.

Then, as now, there were so many talented women in business, politics, technology and the not-for-profit sector that were making a difference but they were still 'under the radar.' We published the result of that conversation 18 months later, a paperback of their bios titled **Women Worth Knowing.** It did a fine job of profiling these bright women rising in their careers. The book also helped many of the most interesting women in our area market their skills and network effectively.

Flash ahead to another summer afternoon, sipping wine and talking about work and what might be needed. We landed on another project idea to help another group of ambitious people. As the owner of a company that provides management training, I'd been relating how many facilitators and speakers say they need a book, but are in the dark about how to get it.

These speakers and course leaders already recognize that a well-written book would add to their credibility while delivering their messages to a broader base. Yet finding the time and know-how to bring their books to market eluded them.

My own area of strength is training solutions. I couldn't answer their questions. But Jackie could. She'd ghost-written and taken to market a number of books. The conversation turned to the challenges and practicalities of the process for experts in various fields who need a book to promote themselves and share their knowledge.

Several months later, Jackie emailed me to say she'd given our conversation a lot of thought and had written the book that could fill that 'I-need-a-book gap.' Would I like to read it? My reading pile is usually precariously balanced, but with a request from her, I agreed.

To my surprise the book is an easy read. While completely informative for anyone considering using a ghostwriter to write their book, it weighs out the advantages of sticking to what you do best and letting someone else tell your story. Jackie combines the how-to info with interesting examples of ghostwritten books (like Trump's **The Art Of The Deal**), how to avoid some of the costly mistakes in book creation and step-by-step ideas on where to go for writers, how to evaluate them, what you can expect to pay and even some great advice on how to contract with the various people you need to get your book written, printed and distributed.

If you are thinking of putting your ideas into a book, check this one out first. It will save you time and money and help you get your book successfully to market.

Enjoy a good read....

Dale Wilcox, CTDP

Dale Wilcox is President and Owner of Watmec (www.watmec.com), an international supplier of customized, effective and actionable learning interventions for progressive companies that drive strategic alignment, engage learners and lead to tangible business benefits.

Just to say THANKS for reading **Get Your Book Written**, I'd like to give you the **Get Your Book Written Workbook**, 100% FREE!

The workbook provides all the lists included in this book – it's the starting point for planning your book!

Go to

www.johnsonbookghostwriting.com/ GYBW-Bonus/

"There is no immortality but the opinion we leave in the minds of men." [1]

- Napoleon Bonaparte, Emperor of France

[1] David McCullough and David Grubin, Empires: Napoleon, PBS (series created for American public broadcasting network), 2000.

Get Your Book Written

ONE | You Need a Powerfully-Written Book

A published book can stake out your territory, influence your audience, enhance your reputation and even alter your destiny. It allows you to present yourself as you wish the world to see you, using your words to portray your point of view.

You can author the non-fiction book that will change your life at almost any age; early in adulthood, at mid-career or later. This is true whether you're starting out in your career or avocation, moving in a new direction, or need a platform to shed light on your life's challenges and victories.

This book is about the fastest, easiest and most efficient method there is to get your business book written and out there, in the hands and before the eyes of the readers you want to inform, enthrall and impress.

Armed with this information, you could be reading your own book by this time next year. Or sooner.

In **Get Your Book Written**, we'll consider how, with the help of a professional writing collaborator, you will get the book you need that readers will welcome and respond to.

The information and advice in this book applies whether your book is directed to potential clients and colleagues or a broader audience of mainstream readers...whether it illuminates a topic related to your career or your passion project or cause...whether your aim is to inform and inspire or simply leave a record for the next generation of leaders in your business.

The Mission: create the book you will be proud of.

The Vision: Make a significant and recognized contribution to your peers and your industry.

The Strategy: Work with a collaborator/ghostwriter, and perhaps other professionals, to create the book that will enhance your professional status, attract new opportunities and help you take your rightful place as a thought leader.

The Payoff: Create the ready-to-publish non-fiction book that will expand your network, enhance your reputation, propel your career and attract new opportunities.

What one thing can you do this year that will change your life?

What will you do this year that will give you increased status, money and success? What one thing could make your life better, richer, fuller and more meaningful?

Perhaps you have a few possibilities in mind. For example, you could be featured in a cover story in an influential magazine, such as *Forbes, Vogue, Time* or *The Economist.*

Or you could host a television documentary about your area of expertise or interest.

You might set out to meet the five most influential people in your industry or area of interest.

You could do everything it takes to win a major award in your field.

You could achieve any one of the items on your Life Bucket List. Maybe more than one.

But of all these choices, the one that is most accessible, available and do-able now, for almost anyone, is this: You could author your book.

This one choice is so potent it could lead to more quickly and easily achieving any of the other goals on this list. Being a published author opens windows and doors to other opportunities that, right now, may seem to be beyond your grasp.

A well-written book has a magnetic power of attraction for whatever it is you really want in life.

The power of being an influencer

If you have information, data, ideas, stories and values to share, there is no better way to do it than between the covers of a well-written book.

Other modern media, such as articles, podcasts, blog posts and short videos, are as transitory as the leaves of autumn. Here today, by tomorrow they're scattered by the wind into the vastness of the landscape.

While emails get deleted and newspapers or magazines go into the recycling bin, people rarely toss a book. They read it, keeping it to re-read or passing it along to another reader. In a too-loud, too-busy, too-crowded world, books still get noticed. Books command respect in any landscape.

Books, more than any other medium, shape the agenda.

Some books make money for their authors; most don't. While having a book that is another source of income would be a welcome benefit for most authors, gaining book sales for your book isn't the main point. More important is the new opportunities that will open for you directly because you are a published author. Some of these opportunities could be very lucrative.

A book has the authority, heft and power to be the tree, not the leaves. A book endures.

You can use your book to leverage your vision, your mission and your brand. As BJ Gallagher said on HuffPost recently, writing a book "makes you an 'expert' without having a Ph.D. or university affiliation.

"Even if you lose money on the book, it can still be worth it in terms of increasing your fees, building your client base, selling more of whatever your product is and building a name for yourself in your chosen field." [2]

---

[2] B. J. Gallagher, "The Ten Awful Truths – and the Ten Wonderful Truths – About Book Publishing," *Huffington Post*, June 5, 2012. www.huffingtonpost.com/bj-gallagher/book-publishing_b_1394159.html

A published book is both an achievement and a status symbol, like having earned an advanced degree or certification in your profession.

A book will extend your network, which in turn will foster new partnerships.

A book will touch the lives of people you will never meet. Imagine getting calls or emails from people whose lives are changed for the better because of your book.

When it happens, it touches your heart as few other experiences ever can. This is, frankly, one of my own major reasons for writing this book.

More benefits of becoming an author

The process of creating a book also has other benefits. It can help you clarify your thoughts. The process of book creation requires self-knowledge and self-reflection. It requires you to clearly state, perhaps for the first time, your mission and your unique brand.

Almost anyone can write a book, with time and effort. Using a professional ghostwriter is likely to be your most expensive option – but also the fastest.

As André Agassi said of the process of writing his book, **Open**, about his professional tennis career, "I wanted to see my own narrative come into focus." [3] In working with writer J. R. Moehringer, Agassi's own meaning in life came into focus. The book gives readers ringside seats to Agassi's rebirth as human being – not merely a tennis-playing robot, which is

------

[3] *Charles McGrath, "A Team, but Watch How You Put It," November 12, 2009, Books, The New York Times. www.nytimes.com/2009/11/12/books/12agassi.html*

what makes **Open** so much more compelling than just another ghosted jock memoir.

While a well-written article can offer snapshots of such a process, a book has the length and depth to present the entire story.

If you have new information to share, a different and compelling perspective or a new take on a trending or popular subject, a moving personal story of triumph over adversity, a cautionary tale to tell, you need a book.

Who will write my book?

It could be true that the person who writes your book should not be you. Here are the reasons for choosing to work with a ghostwriter:

1. Consider: Do I have the time to write a book?

If you're a busy manager, speaker or entrepreneur, ask yourself: What would I have to sacrifice to make time to write this book? Consider that writing a book requires many steps. As an author, I can tell you that it always takes more time than you think it will, or think it should, to write, re-write and polish a book manuscript.

The book that seems so effortless to read, so easy to write, never is. It is part of the craft to make a book or any creative work appear effortless.

What you see in any completed book or other creative work is the graceful dancing swan, not the dancer's bleeding feet.

What will you sacrifice to make your book a reality?

Consider that writing a book can take a year, perhaps longer. It is work that requires blocks of time and total concentration, not something you can do in scraps of time in your day or while doing something else, such as driving. It could take years to complete your book working in your spare time.

What would you need to sacrifice to do this?

Time with family and friends? Other responsibilities? Getting enough sleep? Going to the gym? Taking that next course or getting that next certification you need for career advancement? Using all your vacation time or taking a leave of absence to get your book done? Passing on other attractive opportunities, because you need to get this book out of your head, onto the page and out to your readers?

And here's another issue to consider: Do you really want to take on a book project on your own?

2. Consider: Are your skills more profitably directed elsewhere?

Consider the true value of your time and the opportunity cost of writing a book.

What would it cost you to take a year or so away from your career to write this book?

There would be lost income and bonuses. You'd have a year of living on savings. You would possibly lose a year's pension contributions along with other benefits of employment such as insurance. There might be conferences or other networking opportunities that you'd miss out on.

Consider that a year is a long time to be out of action, as far as your colleagues and competitors are concerned. Would you be able to return and simply pick up where you left off? Today, in most businesses and industries, the answer is no, you couldn't.

When you do the math, it could be that hiring a professional ghostwriter is going to save you more than money.

There are the costs you can't state in dollars, pounds or any other currency. Think about the stress of taking on another major project, one outside your own expertise. There could be a time-consuming learning curve. Writing on a professional level is one of those skills that, unlike most other creative pursuits, is almost entirely self-taught, mainly by trial and error. Do you have the time to teach yourself how to write a quality book?

What would you miss out on during those long hours toiling away on your book? What strain would it put on your marriage (or any relationship), family life and friendships? What lasting regrets could this cause?

What if, instead, you used this time to do other things that enhance your life, either your professional life or personal life? This might be public speaking, networking, teaching, mentoring or volunteering.

It could also be enjoying more quality leisure time to rest and recharge. Perhaps pursuing a new hobby. Having more time for reading, sports, travel...whatever you want more of in your life.

You may decide using a ghostwriter will be more cost-effective, cause less stress and be a faster path too a better result than writing it yourself.

3. You're not a writer, and don't want to be:

Many people who might have enough raw talent to become professional writers are far more productive, fulfilled and possibly more prosperous as:

- lawyers (solicitors, barristers, attorneys or advocates)
- doctors
- politicians
- bureaucrats
- entrepreneurs
- managers
- inventors
- scientists
- educators

If you're a poor writer (and you know it), a good writer (but don't really enjoy spending hours writing) or a good-plus (even great) writer, you still might not be the right writer for your book.

It could be that someone with a fresh eye, skilled at getting to the heart of the story and telling that story with flair is going to do a better job than you can. The objectivity they bring to your topic is just one of the benefits of delegating the writing of your book to a professional book ghostwriter.

4. Do you need to delegate?

Not to your overworked assistant, your friend the struggling screenwriter, or the kid next door who helped with your website, because they are unlikely to create the strong book you need.

A professional book writer has the skills, experience and professionalism to convert your desire to author a book and your raw material into the polished, professional writing readers expect from you. They will help you get your book into the hands of waiting readers in a reasonable amount of time.

No matter which method you choose to get your book written, it takes a high-performance team to create a strong book. Each team member contributes what he or she does best. Here are some of those skills (we talk about each in detail in coming chapters) that book creation requires:

1. The ability to develop a book topic and theme that has legs – readers want this information now.
2. Storytelling ability – readers love a good story!
3. Other writing abilities most often seen in fiction writing: skills with dialogue, pacing, writing hooks and cliffhangers to make your book interesting.
4. Research ability, including interviewing skills
5. Ability to structure a book into a logical, cohesive whole
6. Writing the book
7. Editing for continuity, flow, accuracy and for spelling, grammar and punctuation.
8. Writing the book Introduction or Preface, Bibliography and Footnotes (if needed)

And possibly:

9. Book indexing
10. Writing the cover copy
11. Writing the listing for the book sites such as Amazon, Kobo and Nook.
12. Writing a page about the book for your website or Face Book page.

13. And there are other tasks, depending on if you plan to self-publish. (we'll consider these in another chapter.)

A strong book needs a strong manuscript ready to go to your publisher if you will have one. Some of the above is done before the manuscript goes to the publisher; some as your manuscript is made ready to publish. If you opt to self-publish, you will be doing all these tasks, or hiring them done.

While the world already has a surplus of books, there will never be too many helpful, intelligent, inspiring and well-crafted books, like the book you want to create and your audience hungers for.

"Intimacy is the currency of memoir, and to preserve that feeling of direct access, the ghost's job is, quite literally, to disappear." [4]

- Maureen O'Connor, writing in New York Magazine

---

[4] *Maureen O'Connor, "How to Write Someone Else's Memoir," New York Magazine, September 24, 2015. www.nymag.com/thecut/2015/09/how-to-write-someone-elses-memoir.html*

TWO | What Is a Ghostwriter? What Do They Write?

The day Charlie Miller [5] fell hard during a skiing holiday, a thunderbolt of pain shot from his left hip to his ankle. It was the beginning of the end for his pro career.

He'd been injured before, but never as seriously as this. At just 27, the only career he'd ever wanted was over.

With legions of fans and friends, Charlie was a born doer, not a dreamer. But what did he want to do next?

A friend was starting a wine-making venture and invited Charlie to become a partner. A political party wanted him to run for office. A sports-related charity asked him to be their fundraising manager.

None of these offers grabbed him.

With an uncertain future, he went back to school, completing the undergrad pro sport had interrupted. He volunteered to

---

[5] *Names and some details are changed to protect confidentiality.*

help coach a kids' softball team and football at the local high school. He taught at a summer sports camp. He took more courses and collected a teaching certificate.

Now 32, Charlie was married and had just become a father for the first time. And he was back at his old high school, supply-teaching gym and coaching the football, hockey, track and swim teams on a two-term contract.

It was, next to playing himself, the best job he'd ever had.

Even better, it looked like the senior teacher he'd replaced wouldn't be returning. He'd already been told privately by the principal that he was a strong candidate.

With a wife on maternity leave, a mortgage and most of the money he'd earned in his 20s tied up in investments or already spent, Charlie didn't just want this teaching job. He longed for the stability it could provide.

But teaching jobs, good ones, are as rare as being first draft pick in the first round. There'd be keen competition. He'd need every advantage.

Lost in thought, Charlie barely nodded when Vice-Principal Joanna McCall walked into the staffroom one October afternoon. "Glad I caught you here," she said, noticing the circles under his eyes.

"Baby keeping you up?" she asked, taking a seat. With three teenagers of her own, she could still remember the mind-numbing exhaustion of being a new parent.

"Something like that," Charlie said with a wan smile. "Sorry...just tired..."

"They do learn to like sleeping at night as much as we do, you know," she said.

He shrugged. "I suppose...I mean, yeah, I hope so..."

"And Sallie's well? The baby's OK?"

"Both great," he said, looking up. "Thankfully..."

"Good. But that's not what's on your mind, is it?"

Charlie sighed.

"I think I might know what this problem is. Your degree work is done, all but the thesis. True?" *Stone around my neck*, Charlie thought. It was the final degree requirement he'd hardly paid attention to until he found out that no thesis meant no degree. And no degree meant no teaching job.

"I've done the reading. Got the research organized, but..."

"But you can't put it into words?" He wasn't the only bright student she'd ever taught who simply couldn't get his thoughts and ideas down on paper in an organized way for even as much as an essay question. No wonder the thesis, so like a book and written in academic style, was defeating him.

"That's about it," he said. "I try, but...well, I don't know. Can't get it to all hang together and make sense, or something..."

Joanna asked a few pointed questions, listened closely to his answers, then nodded. "I see. It seems to me that you've done the work, you know your topic and your conclusions, but you just need help putting it into the format and style of a thesis. So, what's needed is a ghostwriter. Leave it with me...I have an idea. I'll get back to you in day or two." With a friendly pat on the arm, she was gone.

Good, Joanna thought, making her way through crowded halls to her office. Popular with students and the other teachers, Charlie had quickly made a place for himself here. Teachers as skilled, passionate and committed as Charlie Miller didn't come along often enough. Both as a colleague and administrator, she wanted to see him join their staff permanently. And she had a plan to make it happen that just might work.

Heading out to the field to do some running drills with the grade nines, Charlie wondered what Ms. McCall – he still had a hard time calling her Joanna – meant by "an idea?"

And just what was a ghostwriter?

Ghostwriter, defined

A ghostwriter is a professional writer hired to write anonymously for a named author, telling that author's story and presenting the author's information in the author's voice.

That is, getting both the message and the words right, in the right order and style, in a way that readers will respond to, writing as if the author is speaking.

Some ghostwriters specialize in writing books, while others are hired by executives to write case studies, white papers, articles, blog posts, annual reports, web content and many other forms of writing, including academic reports, catalog listings and even series of Twitter tweets.

Just about everything beyond a grocery list can and is written by professional ghostwriters.

Some ghosts write theses or dissertations for university degree candidates. Many universities frown on this practice. They are concerned that students do their own work and earn their degrees. Clearly, by anyone`s definition, it is cheating to buy a ready-made research paper or report and call it your own work.

But buying a completed term paper, thesis or dissertation is quite different from enlisting a professional writer's help to get the writing into the correct academic style, tone and format, as Joanna McCall explained to Charlie Miller.

"But is it, well, is it fair?" Charlie asked. "Is it honest?" He'd never been a cheat; never would be.

"I think there's a fine line," she said. "Certainly, if I discovered a student simply bought a completed paper, it would get an F and they'd deserve to fail. But your situation is different, isn't it? You've done the work. This is your research, your insights, your conclusions. And you're ready to defend your thesis in front of your thesis committee.

"You've done what matters, which is the critical thinking showing mastery of a particular problem related to your topic. You own it. It's just that your thesis is still in your head, not on paper. So, here's what I suggest we do..."

Moments later, leaving Joanna's office, Charlie felt as if he'd just been hauled out of a rough ocean and into a lifeboat. A crazy idea, but maybe, just maybe, this could work. He'd get the thesis done, defend it, get his degree...he already felt a glimmer of confidence returning.

Who needs ghostwriters?

Truthfully, the answer would be shorter if you asked, "Who doesn't need ghostwriters?"

But here is a list of those who do use the services of ghostwriters to further their ambitions and their careers:

- Everyone who advertises. Writers and artists who create advertising and marketing messages are very rarely credited, like all the other specialized skills required to create advertising.

- Businesses that need annual reports, materials to motivate their sales teams, speeches or briefing notes for executives and other writing that is usually credited to a manager, but written by a staff member or freelance ghostwriter.
- Corporate trainers, seminar leaders and motivational speakers.
- Politicians.
- Doctors, particularly specialists.
- Scientists and historians.
- Lawyers and judges.
- Event planners.
- Leaders of populist movements, such as conservationists.
- Not-for-profit organizations and agencies and anyone with a cause to publicize.
- Lobbyists and members of think tanks.
- Fund-raisers.
- Interior designers and others in creative and lifestyle retail and related industries.
- Academic leaders, professors and teachers.
- People in service industries, such as investment advisors, real estate agents, mortgage brokers and interior designers.
- Anyone with an unusual, thrilling or uplifting 'true life' story of adventure, escape, spiritual awakening or survival.

These people may not know they need a book ghostwriter, but they probably do:

- Career-changers seeking a foothold in the world of their new career.
- New and recent graduates who want to stand apart from the swarm of candidates seeking the same positions they're aiming to win.
- Anyone who wants to leap up the ladder in their career.
- Anyone who wants to be chosen for a plum volunteer post, win a grant, a fellowship or other big opportunity, such as being invited onto the board of directors of a major company – one that rewards their directors handsomely.
- Anyone who wants to be invited to give a speech, a series of seminars or teach a course.
- Anyone who wants to build their platform.
- Any entrepreneur who needs more leads.

Ghostwriting is everywhere in the real world...

Ghostwriting is much more widespread and popular than many people realize. Look on any list of non-fiction bestsellers today and half of the books there, perhaps more, are ghostwritten.

The practice has become so common that very few celebrities or politicians write their own books. It simply makes more sense to hire it done and get on with whatever it is that makes them famous.

This isn't a recent phenomenon. For centuries, those who can afford to hire book ghostwriting have taken advantage of this powerful tool.

Here are some examples showing you the variety of books written for their authors by ghostwriters.

In 1816, Napoleon Bonaparte wrote his memoirs. Of the millions of words written about him in his own century and since, Napoleon in his own words remains the most revealing, forceful and compelling insight into who he was, what he did and why.

His book would be his final battle plan. It was designed to reaffirm his contributions, anchor his legacy, shape his message and myth and assure he could never be forgotten. In all of this, his book succeeded.

Today, we'd say the former Emperor of France was masterful in managing his personal brand, with the help of his ghostwriter, aide and friend, Emmanuel Las Cases.

While many others have written books about Napoleon the soldier, the strategist, the ruler, the reformer and the man, none could be as revealing as what was written in his own voice.

Master of horror fiction H. P. Lovecraft was the ghostwriter behind Harry Houdini's **Imprisoned With The Pharaohs**. Written in 1924, it uses the famous magician and escape artist as the lead character. Houdini was happy with the book, but their second novel was never published. Houdini died in 1926, before it was completed.

His widow did not want the book published and the manuscript vanished. However, it turned up in some old papers found in a magicians' supply shop in 2016, and is now in the hands of private collectors. A case of the fate of the manuscript of a ghosted book being just as dramatic as the story it tells.

Before winning fame writing westerns and screenplays under his own name, along with both Pulitzer and Academy Awards, Larry McMurtry was a prolific ghostwriter. Best-known of his ghosted books is **Daughter Of The Tejas** by Ophelia Ray. [6]

Sinclair Lewis became both rich and famous for **Main Street**, but before that he paid his bills ghostwriting biographies such as Maurice McLoughlin's **Tennis As I Play It**. [7]

Acclaimed British poet and novelist Robert Graves signed his own name to the Forward of **Old-Soldier Sahib**, by his friend Frank Richards. Graves, whose own novels have never been out of print, also ghosted Richards' book.

Ellery Queen was both a fictional detective and the writing name of cousins Daniel Nathan and Emanuel Benjamin Lepofsky, who created the Ellery Queen series of novels and *Ellery Queen Magazine*, hugely popular in the 1930s and 1940s. Many other writers were the ghosts behind the Ellery Queen byline, including writers famous for science-fiction under their own names including Theodore Sturgeon, Auram Davidson and Jack Vance.

Pulitzer Prize winning short story and novel author Katherine Anne Porter's first published book was the one she ghosted: **My Chinese Marriage** by Mae Franking.

---

[6] *Scott Laming, "Top 10 Ghostwritten Books," undated. www.abebooks.com/books*

[7] *Maurice McLoughlin (1890 to 1957) was the best American tennis player of his generation. His friend Sinclair Lewis ghosted his book, Tennis As I Play It, published in 1915.*

Like Ellery Queen, the named authors of both the Nancy Drew and Hardy Boys mystery series for young readers never actually existed. Both series were written by many writers under the publishers' house names of Carolyn Keene and Franklin W. Dixon. [8]

Hedy Lamarr objected to the book written for her but without her input by Leo Guild, **Ecstasy And Me: My Life As A Woman**. She sued the publisher claiming that what Guild had written was more invented fiction than fact, particularly some lurid details about her love life. The controversy as well as the scandalous content helped sell even more copies of the book.

John F. Kennedy was a rising young senator when he got the idea for the book that became **Profiles In Courage**. It won the Pulitzer Prize in 1957, proclaimed his place in the sun as Influencer and helped get him elected as Governor of Texas, then President of the United States.

---

[8] *Both the Nancy Drew and Hardy Boys mystery series for young readers were written to supplied templates and plotlines by several ghostwriters. The Nancy Drew books were published under the pen name of Carolyn Keene. The Hardy Boys books' author was the equally fictional Franklin W. Dixon.*

Mildred Wirt Benson wrote the first Nancy Drew book, and another 22 of the first 30 titles published. Today there are more than 500 titles in the Nancy Drew series. Leslie McFarlane wrote the first 18 books in the Hardy Boys series. Both series were the invention of Edward Stratemeyer, who also devised the characters and plots for these series: The Rover Boys, The Bobbsey Twins, Tom Swift, Baseball Joe and The Dana Girls. During his lifetime, (1862 to 1930) these series sold a total 5 million copies, making him one of the most successful publishers of all time. He also wrote 1,300 books under his own name.

But Kennedy didn't write the book. His ghostwriter was Ted Sorensen, a Kennedy aide and speechwriter. [9]

Hillary Clinton has authored four books of memoirs with the help of ghostwriters. Her first book was **It Takes A Village: And Other Lessons Children Teach Us**, written by Barbara Feinman Todd, a university journalism professor who wasn't credited. The book was reportedly edited by Ms. Clinton and perhaps others before publication. [10]

Her most recent memoir, **Hard Choices**, was written with the help of three advisors she calls her "book team," who are named near the end of her 702-page book. [11]

Merle Ginsberg took just five weeks to co-author Paris Hilton's 2004 best-seller, **Confessions Of An Heiress**. The rush was on because the publisher wanted to capitalize on Hilton's popularity at the time. [12]

Sheryl Sandberg credits journalist Nell Scovell as her "writing partner" in her Acknowledgements for **Lean In**; Scovell is the ghostwriter.

Naomi Judd's book about overcoming personal adversity, **River Of Time: My Descent Into Depression And How I**

---

[9] *Paul Farhi, "Who wrote that political memoir? No, who actually wrote it?" The Washington Post, June 9, 2014. https://www.dawn.com/news/1112219/who-wrote-that-political-memoir-the-pens-behind-the-politicians*

[10] *David D. Kirkpatrick, "Media Talk: Mrs. Clinton Seeks Ghostwriter for Memoirs," The New York Times, January 8, 2001.*

[11] *Paul Farhi, op cit.*

[12] *Maureen O'Connor, op cit.*

Emerged With Hope was written by ghost Marcia Wilke, who specializes in celebrity bios.

Donald Trump's first book, **The Art Of The Deal**, was written with and, reportedly, entirely by Tony Schwartz. Schwartz, then a journalist published in *The New Yorker* and *The New York Times*, also supplied the theme for the Trump book and the title. That book led to creation of Trump's reality TV program, *The Apprentice* which was a major factor in building his popular support for election, in 2016, as President of the United States. [13]

Bestseller **Shoe Dog** by Nike co-founder and Board Chair Phil Knight was written with the help of ghostwriter J. R. Moehringer, a novelist and former *Los Angeles Times* journalist who won a Pulitzer in 2000 for newspaper feature writing. Bill Gates (of Microsoft fame) chose **Shoe Dog** as one of his Best Books of 2016. [14]

Moehringer was also the writer behind tennis star André Agassi's memoir, **Open**, published in 2009.

Gary Erikson chose author and social ethics professor Lois Lorentzen to write **Raising The Bar** about how he turned a homemade granola bar into international brand Clif Bar.

Like writing duo Ellery Queen, some contemporary fiction writers are so popular they can't possibly write books fast

---

[13] Jane Mayer, "Donald Trump's Ghostwriter Tells All," New Yorker Magazine, July 25, 2016. www.newyorker.com/magazine/2016/07/25/donald-trumps-ghostwriter-tells-all

[14] Bill Gates, "My Favorite Books of 2016," December 5, 2016. https://www.gatesnotes.com/About-Bill-Gates/Best-Books-2016

enough to meet readers' demands or to use all their storylines about characters or 'worlds' they've created.

One of these is Tom Clancy. His **Splinter Cell** books were written by David Michaels, pen name for writer Raymond Benson, also known for writing some of the most recent novels in the James Bond series. [15]

Since gothic fiction writer V.C. Andrews' death in 1986, ghostwriter Andrew Neiderman has continued to write novels under her name and using her writing style. Neiderman is also the author of 44 thrillers under his own name. [16]

Ghostwriter Kirstie McLellan Day had already scored a hat trick of bestselling sports memoirs with Theoren Fleury's **Playing With Fire** (2009), Bob Probert's **Tough Guy** (2010) and Ron MacLean's **Cornered** (2011). Her most recent hockey memoir is written with all-time top scoring player Wayne Gretzky. **99 Stories Of The Game** was published in 2016. [17]

Are There Ghosts in Academia?

Yes. Professors come up with research ideas and analyze results, but most are far too busy to do their own writing because of limited time or they haven't developed book writing skills. They rarely choose to write journal articles reporting their latest findings. Instead, they rely on research assistants and graduate students as their journal article ghostwriters. It's also common (and a widely-accepted

---

[15] *http://mentalfloss.com/article/12689/your-favorite-authors-are-frauds-6-famous-ghostwriters*

[16] *Andrew Neiderman, www.neiderman.com*

[17] *Shelley Youngblut, "Kirstie McLellan Day: Hockey's leading muse," The Globe and Mail, May 15, 2012*

practice) for academics to hire professional book ghostwriters to describe their breakthroughs for a wider audience.

Both product brands and personal brands need to be developed, honed and marketed. This requires the skills of many types of experts, none of whom are named. The person who conceives and storyboards an ad, who writes that ad, who voices it for television or radio, or who creates the photos or video or graphics and layout if it is a print ad, who edits it...all these people are well-paid yet uncredited, performing work-for-hire.

When the president or CEO of a company shares her thoughts in a message in the annual report, or gives a speech to peers at a convention, no one expects her to write the words. We know they are the work of an annual report ghostwriter or a speech ghostwriter.

It doesn't seem reasonable to expect the executive who did not write his or her own speech or advertisement to sit down and write their own book.

But Is Ghostwriting Legal?

Yes, when the work or the book truly represents the thinking and ideas of the author.

There is a clear line between fiction and non-fiction. While there are ghostwriters or collaborators who specialize in writing romances, mysteries or other fiction, this book is focussed on writing business nonfiction books.

Your book may be a memoir or an autobiography. A biography is about a person (or product or company). The autobiography is told in first person. It is inside the head of the author (or subject), not told from the outside looking in.

She, he or they did this -- is biography.

I or we did this -- is autobiography or memoir.

What should your book be about?

Sometimes, authors have a clear, well-defined book concept in mind. More often, they need help firming up the idea to get the best, brightest, most marketable book concept. That is, it is as appealing to readers, delivering the most information, insight and entertainment (most well-written non-fiction books are a combo of these three).

Your book needs to promise big, then over-deliver on your big promise (we'll talk more about this soon).

Your ghostwriter may provide the service of helping you define - and refine - your book topic and theme (as I do for my authors). Your ghostwriter may even come up with the title and subtitle of your book. They will be responsible for organizing the book, giving it the best structure to suit both you and the content. They write, re-write, polish the manuscript and might also edit it and do some of the research.

Some ghostwriters offer additional services, from initial idea all the way to publishing your book and delivering print copies. For others, their role is done when you receive the completed manuscript and accept it.

The experiences, stories, thinking, 'personality' or brand and possibly bonus content such as checklists – that is, all the meat and veg of the book – come from the named author. It's the writer that cooks it and plates it up to entice and satisfy a hungry reader.

When a ghostwritten book is fiction, the author (or their publisher) supplies specific guidelines to the ghostwriter including voice, tone, characters and sometimes a plot outline and book title.

For a non-fiction ghostwritten book, you as the author supply your insights in:

- Interviews with your collaborator/writer. These are usually recorded and transcribed.
- Articles written by or about you
- Lists of publications, degrees, certificates or other qualifications, awards and honours
- Recordings of your podcast, TV, or radio interviews
- Lists of other sources such as colleagues or friends and family to be interviewed and their contact information
- Lists of books you admire. It also helps if you tell your ghostwriter what it is, specifically, that you like about these book examples.

For more help preparing to start your book with a ghostwriter, see the **Get Your Book Written Workbook** – which you can download for free with the purchase of this book.

Most writers, want a lot of supplied research and background material – the more, the better. We ghostwriters spend a big chunk of pre-writing time pouring over all this material to get a deep and complete understanding of who you are. All this material is returned to you at the end of the project.

Before starting to write, you and your ghostwriter need a deep understanding of:

- Who you are, professionally and as a person? What is unique about you, your experiences, skills and outlook?
- What will this book uniquely reveal about you and your product or company or achievements?

- What is your essential message?
- What are your strengths?
- Who are the readers for your message? What do they care about? What problems do they need to solve?
- What action do you want your reader to take as a result of reading your book?
- How will this book fit with everything else you're doing to proclaim your personal brand?
- How will this book help you build your network and platform?
- How will this book fit with other books you've written or want to write in the future?

The book truly does belong to you, the person whose name is on the cover. A skilled professional book ghostwriter will do everything in his or her power, using an arsenal of tools, to vanish behind the showcased author of the book, becoming what a ghostwriter should be – invisible.

Sometimes, authors choose to partially share credit for the book, turning their ghostwriter into a co-writer. For example, on the cover it would say:

By Anthony Author

As told to Grace Ghostwriter

Or

With Grace Ghostwriter

Or they bring their ghostwriter out of the closet with a call-out in the Acknowledgements at the end of the book, for example thanking the writer "for research assistance."

More often, the ghostwriter stays firmly in the background and is not credited. Publishers may know who ghosted a given celebrity's book; literary agents and other book world insiders know, sometimes journalists know this too and report on it. Readers don't know, and often don`t particularly care. What they want is a good read.

Your contract with your ghostwriter will specify how credit will be given, if any, and will also include a non-disclosure or confidentiality clause. (We'll look at contracts and what they include in Chapter Five.)

You are the face, mind, brand, spirit and soul of your book.

In my opinion, your name is the one that should be on the cover and title page.

Ghostwriter J. R. Moehringer agrees, insisting his name never be on the cover or the title page of his authors' books, saying, "the midwife does not go home with the baby." [18]

Is Ghostwriting Ethical?

Before answering, let me ask you:

Is it ethical for Adele, say, or k. d. lang or Michael Bublé to do a cover of a Joni Mitchell song with permission from Ms. Mitchell and payment for the rights?

Is it ethical for Alison Balsom to play the trumpet solo in Haydn's Trumpet Concerto in E Flat in front of an orchestra conducted by Xian Zhang, all these musicians giving voice to Joseph Haydn's notes on the page?

Is it ethical for an actor to say words he didn't write?

---

[18] *Charles McGrath, op cit.*

Is it ethical for a rising young actor to portray Mr. Spock or Captain Kirk in a whole new generation of **Star Trek**, even though other actors created these roles?

Or for Benedict Cumberbatch to portray Sherlock Holmes, even though that character was created by Sir Arthur Conan Doyle and has been portrayed by a long list of actors?

Is it ethical for a portrait artist to accept your commission to paint a picture of you? Is the resulting painting ethical?

I imagine you saying, "Yes, of course," to every one of these questions, likely without needing to give it much thought. We accept that creative people interpret and re-interpret creative works, portraying the spirit and essence of the originators, or perhaps taking startling departures (such as, for example, staging *King Lear* in modern-day Mexico City or with a female actor in the title role).

Ghostwriters or co-writers do the same, channelling their subject or topic, shaping the material, presenting it to both inform and entertain a targeted audience.

Personally, I believe ghostwriting is an art, a craft and an honourable service, both to authors and readers when practiced in an honest and ethical way.

Ghostwriting specialties

Most ghostwriters specialize, even within a format. So, for example, professional non-fiction book ghostwriters may exclusively write sports memoirs and may even specialize in one sport. They may choose to write celebrity bios or the biographies of politicians, books about science and technology breakthroughs, business leadership or may only take assignments about a specific topic or industry.

Often ghostwriters are also known for writing under their own names, as book writers or journalists.

Both journalists and book writers need to be competent wordsmiths. But their skills need to go far beyond a deft touch with words. As both a former newspaper and magazine journalist and a former journalism teacher, let me list 10 critical skills both journalists and book ghostwriters need in order be successful:

1. **Both journalists and book writers must be able to recognize a 'hot' article or book idea when they see it**. They understand what will interest, inform and enthrall readers. They know how to turn almost any topic, even the most seemingly dry or mundane, into something people will take the time to read. They are aware of current events and read widely themselves.

2. **They know how to interview**. They're good at finding sources and getting them to talk. They're skilled at spotting the telling details, what some writing teachers call the Golden Nuggets of the story to delight readers. Golden Nuggets are the sometimes odd or quirky facts, quotes and other little gifts, like a clever turn of phrase, that reward and satisfy readers. Golden Nuggets are to writing what herbs or spices are in a delicious dish.

3. **Deadlines are set in stone**. A writer who doesn't internalize this rule won't last long as a journalist, for whom deadlines are constant and relentless. Among magazine and book writers, meeting or exceeding deadlines is a mark of professionalism.

4. **Self-directed**. They don't want, or need, handholding or an author (or anyone else) looking over their shoulder. They know what they're doing and want to

get on with it. They take the initiative to tell the best story in the best possible way.

5. **They're a quick study**. Journalists learn how to 'capture' a topic quickly, gaining enough knowledge to ask intelligent questions when preparing for an interview. They can skim read and absorb information fast. They can also explain complex concepts in straight-forward language so that readers will quickly grasp the meaning, without ever sounding like they are talking down to readers.

6. **Ability to listen deeply**. Concentrated listening results in hearing what is being said – and what's not being said. In most conversations, people are only half-listening to each other. Smart journalists learn to hyper-focus on the person they are talking to, turning the full wattage of their attention on the speaker.

7. **Understanding the structure**. Every article and every book has an internal structure, like the frame of a house. There are many possible structures the writer can choose. For example, the structure of a case study is simple: problem-solution-result.

Some books are simply carefully selected case studies or a series of case studies cleverly tied together. Another possible book structure is chronological, an 'as-it-happened' approach to the topic. Or a book could focus entirely on one period of life (childhood and adolescence, for example) or one milestone (what happened the year an author became number one in the world in a certain skill).

There is a whole buffet table of possible structures to choose from. A skilled book ghostwriter knows how to recognize which is the structure that will best serve your readers and your message.

8. **Storytelling that grabs readers**. Every book needs to tell stories. There are many reasons for this, but the one that matters the most is that readers love stories and can't ever get enough of them. (For more about storytelling, see Chapter Seven).

9. **Flawless spelling, punctuation and grammar and correct word choice**. This one should be a given but, sadly, it isn't. Computer spell-checkers and grammar-checkers can't be relied upon, either. They can catch problems, but they can also introduce mistakes.

10. **Good communicators**. Professional writers of all stripes write concise emails and return emails or calls promptly.

In short, they are the kind of people everyone wants to work with: skilled professionals who know what they're doing and deliver competent work.

What truly does not matter in choosing your ghostwriter?

Here are a few things that will make very little or no difference in working with a professional book ghostwriter:

1. **Location** – either theirs, or yours. Some writers want to meet with their author partners, even moving in with them and literally shadowing their authors for weeks or even months. This 'Up Close and Personal' intensive approach adds expense to the project as well as consuming time.

   Today, with phone, e-mail and computer-enhanced communication (such as Skype), you and your ghostwriter don't need to live in the same city, or even in the same country. So long as work gets done to schedule and deadlines and expectations are met, it really doesn't matter where you live, or where your ghostwriter lives.

2. **Your Perfect Match ghostwriter** is probably out there somewhere. There are thousands of ghostwriters who you could choose; among them likely a hundred (at least) who could do a superb job of your book. Don't put off getting started while you wait for The One.

3. **Compatible hours of work and work styles.** It doesn't matter if your ghostwriter prefers to write from midnight to dawn, or early mornings, or all afternoon, or in their bathrobe. If the work is done to your satisfaction, it doesn't matter. Ghosts don't have a dress code or punch a timeclock. Some writers are nine-to-five types, but not many I know of. Agree on when and how they will return phone calls and e-mails, and other than that, let them get on with it.

4. **Likeability is a nice to have, but not a key factor.** The trust, respect and courtesy must be mutual. You are friendly to each other, but probably won't become friends.

5. **Gender, age, hair colour, sock size**...all irrelevant.

What else do book ghostwriters need to be good at?

Here are some skills that you might not find in even the best journalists, but you'll want and need them to be highly developed in your book ghostwriter:

1. **Project management**. They've written at least one book; know how to do it and how to get it done. They don't get lost in the research or bogged down in details.

They stay on top of the process and work to a plan with deadlines.

2. **Entrepreneurial thinking**. Unless selling your book is not something you want to do (for example, you plan to use it as a promotional gift or it's intended as a memoir for your children and grandchildren only), you need a writer who understands what it takes to sell books, and has the chops to write a book that will sell in the current market.

3. **Patience**. Book writing is a marathon, not the sprint writing an article is. Professional book ghostwriters maintain their energy level and enthusiasm throughout the project, even when (as often happens in the later stages) everyone just wants this book to be done.

4. **Research skills beyond interviewing**. Unless you have done all the research or plan to hire a researcher to work with your ghostwriter, your writer needs research skills. They need to know how to find those 'Golden Nugget' facts or get the quotes that make your book memorable.

5. **Specialists in the type of book you have in mind** – memoir, business book, career guidance or self-help, personal adventure or story of survival. They don't necessarily need to be experts in your specific business or industry. Most pro writers of books know how to be a quick study in any topic.

For example, I write books for executives, speakers, trainers and coaches and on career development and lifestyle/self-help topics. I would hesitate to take on a biography of a sports celebrity, for example, or a hip-hop artist because I don't have a background or understanding of those worlds.

Even with the journalist's ability of being a very quick study, I'm not sure I could capture enough of these worlds to create the authenticity of these authors' voices. Authenticity is one of the deliverables a skilled ghostwriter delivers to their authors.

I'm sure Charlie Miller, the teacher whose story opened this chapter, has a great sports memoir in him, but I wouldn't be the ideal ghostwriter I have little interest in sports.

On the other hand, if he chose to author a book about using pro sports training and motivation techniques to help refugees from war-ravaged countries overcome their trauma and integrate successfully in their new lives or use these same techniques to help soldiers with PTSD or, again, using new ways to help troubled inner-city kids get their lives back on-track, any of these could be a terrific book, one I would happily take on. I know something about these topics and, more importantly, I care about them.

You need passion to power through the inevitable problems and frustrations of a project with many moving parts.

6. **Passion for your topic**. If you ever watch those reality talent contests on TV, you'll have noticed that contestants who just have a good voice or are good dancers never make it to the finals.

The winners are always the people who sing well or dance well because they have dedicated the time and effort to excel. They live it, they breathe it, they are so committed the sheer wattage of their passion reaches right back to the cheap seats. We find it irresistible. We are compelled to stand up and cheer.

That's what we want in your book.

We want that passion, that intensity, that feeling of being fully alive, strong, powerful, in full control.

It's what your reader wants too, shining forth from every page.

Red flags – who NOT to hire as your ghostwriter

With all the above in mind, I hope you now have a clearer picture of the person who will soon be your ghostwriter. But it may also help in your decision to talk about who you will want to avoid.

Here are the danger signs that could mean frustration and difficulty ahead:

1. **Inexperience** – they've never written a published book. Or, worse, they've never written anything that has been published. Ask for writing samples. Ask where they have been published. Check that these are authentic samples, from real publications.
2. **Fuzzy thinking**. Define your book as clearly as possible, as early as possible. All books change and evolve in the writing. However, it is hard to tell where you're going when you don't have a destination to begin with.
3. **Vague promises**. No deliverables. No deadlines.

4. **No contract**. This is too informal an arrangement to expect reliable results. Insist on keeping everything on a businesslike basis.
5. **Too cheap**. Just as when you hire any professional service, you get what you pay for.
6. **No proof** they can deliver a professional quality book manuscript. Ask to see books they have written under their own name.
7. **Poor communication skills**. Unreliable.
8. **Lack of work ethic and lack of other indicators of professionalism**. This is a judgement call you will need to make from their website, your initial conversations and their testimonials.
9. **Lack of respect for readers**. All too commonly, there are writers who fail to treat readers with the respect everyone deserves. Talking down to readers, lecturing them, shoddy or careless work, lazy writing – all these are insulting to readers.
10. **Zero enthusiasm for your topic**. Don't hire a ghostwriter who, it seems to you, is just doing your book to get your money because your message will die on the page. Readers can always tell.
11. **All hat, no overalls**. Don't hire the flashy talker. They usually can't write.

Where to find your ghostwriter

If you already have an agent, or a traditional publisher, or both, they will likely suggest several professional writers. You will have the choice of who you want to work with.

However, this luxury is usually reserved for celebrities, national politicians, royalty and anyone who already has such a strong platform of eager readers that major publishers want the book and big-name ghostwriters are competing for the chance to write it. These writers make top dollar for their work, usually as a cut of the advance.

Few of the thousands of books published each year are written by (or for) celebrities or anyone else whose story is likely to sell in the hundreds of thousands, or even a million-plus copies.

In this century, most first-time authors who do get an agent and/or a publisher interested in their book will be offered only a modest advance against future royalties. These days, most writers are self-published. They write the book themselves or choose and hire their own writing collaborator.

Here's how authors can find ghostwriting partners:

1. Though referrals from friends or colleagues.
2. Through referrals from literary agents or writers' associations.
3. By approaching a journalist, speechwriter or corporate writer in their own organization, or who they know by reputation and whose writing they admire and asking if they know of someone who is a professional book ghostwriter.
4. By approaching the ghostwriter of a book on a similar topic. If the ghostwriter isn't credited, you can sometimes find out who they are by looking in the book's Acknowledgements for someone who is thanked for their help with the research or editing. They might also have been the ghostwriter. Don't ask the author who their ghostwriter is. That's a secret that needs to be kept.
5. By looking online. There are a few agencies that broker ghostwriting (for which the author pays a fee).

Ghostwriters also market their services through their own websites, profiles on LinkedIn, Facebook and other social sites.

What to ask your prospective ghostwriter

Once you have a list of potential ghostwriters for your book, you will want to interview your short-list before you make your hiring decision.

Here's a checklist of questions to ask during these initial conversations:

1. What is your working method? How do you approach a book writing project?
2. What is your usual timeline to deliver a book like the one I have described?
3. What delays do you anticipate?
4. How do you handle disagreements or delays?
5. How long do you usually take to respond to e-mails or phone messages?
6. Can you do the research? Or any additional research that is needed?
7. Do you offer additional services, such as editing, sourcing photos or illustrations, creating graphics, writing cover copy or formatting the final manuscript as an e-book or writing a book proposal for a traditional publisher? If so, what are your fees and timelines for these additional services?

See the **Get Your Book Written Workbook** for more questions to ask your potential ghostwriter – and what answers you want to hear. Instructions to get your copy are at **www.johnsonbookghostwriting.com/gybw-bonus/**

You can expect a professional book ghostwriter to have clear, complete answers to all these questions. They may not initially be able to give you a final cost for their services. Some writers prefer to get started, then re-evaluate the project, based on how complex (and time-consuming) it appears it will be. Some offer a menu of extra services that can quickly increase your cost.

It isn't only about the money...but every book I have ever been involved with has had a budget. This only makes sense.

Back at Trillium High, many of these issues had been discussed by Vice-Principal Joanna McCall and teacher Charlie Miller, who needed to get his thesis done.

"OK," Charlie said. "I see how it could work. Thank you, Joanna. I really appreciate your help. But, well...just one more question. Exactly how much will it cost?"

There's always something you have to give up for success. Everything comes at a cost. Just what are you willing to pay for it?

- Serena Williams, professional tennis player

THREE | What's This Ghostwritten Book Going to Cost?

The scene: home décor store

My mission: Buy cushions for patio chairs.

These blue striped ones would look nice, I think, fingering the fabric. *But will they stand up to family use, including the pets? Not to mention scorching sun, guests who spill, forgetting to bring them in before it rains... Are these cushions up to the challenge for more than just one summer? Probably not,* I decide. *Too flimsy.* I don't bother to check the price.

Further down the aisle another shopper laughs. "I did exactly the same thing," she says. Her cart also remains a empty.

Don't we all do that same thing? Price is usually the last question before making that decision to pop those cushions in the shopping cart...or keep searching.

Quality questions come first

Cushions for outdoor furniture are just a commodity, like socks. Or curtains. Or car seat covers.

We buy them and enjoy them for a while. Then they fade or shrink or the new family pet shreds them, triggering another hunter-gatherer quest for replacements.

Not true for big ticket items, where you confront a host of decisions beyond working through a simple mental checklist of size-colour-quality-price.

Say you're buying a new family car. You've already chosen make and model. But, as with any big-ticket purchase, there are more decisions to make. Lots more. Sunroof or rag-top? Heated leather seats or fabric? Surround sound and a television for the kids in the back or just the basic radio and cd player? Steel alloy wheels? The latest technology in brakes? Custom paint? Extended warranty?

All these options and more are available...for a price that can quickly inflate. You can get exactly what you want (or very close) when you are clear about what you want and are prepared to pay for it.

Or consider the custom kitchen you'd love to have. It's not merely a collection of cabinets, countertops and gleaming new appliances (or fitted kitchen, worktops and gas hob with an American fridge). No, it's the place for your family to gather, cook, eat and entertain. Heart of the home. An emotional decision, justified by how much more this new kitchen will add to your equity, if you decide to upsize. Or the kids move out and you downsize.

The stakes are higher with a bespoke product or service. It takes more thought and more time. More research on your part. Maybe more worry, along with some frustration.

Unlike the patio cushions, you won't decide you want your new car or luxurious new kitchen this morning and have the pleasure and pride of ownership by this afternoon.

At stake are not just the quality level you want, but getting that car, or kitchen specific to your personal needs and desires. Not off the shelf. Not just like those people across the street have. It's all yours and, possibly, uniquely yours.

Like me and almost everyone I know, you probably aren't among the very few people who can ever own an original drawing by Picasso or John Lennon, a previously-unknown original Mozart or Jane Austen script, or Elton John's first piano...but you can have that luxury car or dream kitchen.

Buying the new car or the custom kitchen is a process, not just a purchase.

Big projects all require more effort, cause more aggravation, cost more money and take longer than anyone wants. But all that fades in importance when you take possession and begin to enjoy all the benefits.

So, what does all this have to do with getting the book you want created? My point is this: like the made-in-the-factory-for-you car, or the custom kitchen, you have choices to make about this book you envision. No matter if what you buy is top end, off the shelf or from a charity re-sale shop, you get what you pay for.

Also true when you go shopping for a ghostwriter.

In response to demand, there is a lot of choice on offer in the writer-for-hire marketplace, at just about every price point.

We'll start with the bargain basement option and work our way up to the penthouse sales rooms, where only the elite shop, strictly by invitation only.

These are averages of the amounts quoted by *Writer's Digest*, several writer's associations in the U.S. and Canada, writers I know and who provide their fee ranges on their websites, literary agents and acquisition editors, primarily in the United States. All prices are in U.S. dollars.

Option One: Hire an amateur writer

This will be your riskiest but cheapest ghostwriter option. Amateur writers include the high school or university student who gets good marks in English, the friend-of-a-friend who's always wanted to be a writer, someone who puts up a notice on the bulletin board at the grocery store offering to write student research papers or blog content and the columnist for your local newspaper or the acquaintance who has expertise in your book's topic but has never written anything more than an email.

Any of these people might say they can write your book, but can they back that claim with proof?

The price may be only a few hundred dollars up to a few thousand dollars. The results could be adequate, but odds are against an amateur writer being able to produce the book you'll want your name on.

Option Two: Hire an offshore 'professional' writer

Look online and you will find several services that match people needing writing of various kinds with writers who promise results quickly, for what look like bargain prices.

When I checked, I found several offering to write a book on any topic starting at $ 350.

They usually promise to complete your book in what seems like record time – a few weeks, or just a month.

These writers claim to be native English speakers, and, for some, this is true. But most are writers who live in Asia. They may have been studying English since they were very young. In several Asian countries children are required to learn English in school, while learning most of their subjects in their native languages.

But the English they learn is not native because they don't have the cultural references that you have, as a person who is British, Irish, American, South African, Canadian, Australian or a New Zealander.

Much of what they 'know' of cultural references comes from television programs – mainly American TV.

They are unlikely to be able to write in your voice, with enough knowledge of your subject and directly to your audience. What they write won't sound like you. It will be generic in tone.

There may be mistakes in spelling and grammar. Word choice and sentence structure could be awkward. There will be fluff and lots of repetition to drive up the word count. Their coverage of your topic might not even be skin deep.

As a test, I assigned a simple book topic to a writer I found on one of the freelance worker websites. She is North American, genuinely a native English speaker, assigned a topic related to her university degree.

Her sample writing looked adequate to the task. The book came back to me on time, for the agreed-upon cost. It was on the assigned topic, at the assigned length and delivered most of what I had asked for in the content. But it wasn't publishable.

The writing was flat, the voice a monotone drone, the language lifeless. At first, I thought I could edit it into something readable, smoothing out the rough spots and injecting some body and soul into the manuscript. But what started as editing turned into a ground-up re-write.

If you choose Option Two, you may get a 'good enough' book, perhaps delivering enough information to satisfy your readers. Or you may find that you're going to have to hire a script doctor to resuscitate your manuscript. Or another writer, to start over.

Option Three: Hire a professional writer.

It isn't difficult to find a professional ghostwriter.

Put "professional writer" in the search box of your search engine of choice and you'll get thousands of results, starting with writers who have paid to have their websites listed at the top of page one.

On their websites, they say they can write. They list the publications and clients they have written for. They also may have quotes or testimonials from satisfied customers, a list of their degrees and the writing training they've completed and possibly some writing samples. It all sounds good.

But can they write your book? Possibly. But not if they are a book writing generalist, or if they specialize in a different kind of book writing, such as only doing memoirs when what you have in mind is a book teaching leadership skills.

Another possible problem is they don't write books at all because their specialty is writing marketing copy, annual reports, case studies, blog posts or any of a few dozen other types of Business-to-Business (B2B) or Business-to-Consumer (B2C) writing.

All these forms of professional writing are also ghostwriting.

Each of these has its own formats, conventions, current best practices and rules. Usually, people who can write a sizzling sales letter, or a compelling proposal or a knock-their-socks-off infomercial can't write a good book. Or even a so-so book.

The same is true of talented and successful book writers. Most book ghostwriters can't write an award-winning advertisement or a sales-producing series of emails or a letter that turns prospects into customers. They don't even want to try, because writing each of these, though lucrative, is also a specialty that takes extended time (sometimes years) to master.

Perhaps you'll have the rare good fortune of hiring a 'beginning' book ghostwriter, a talented and ambitious new writer who produces a superb book for you at the low end of the professional ghostwriter fee scale. If so, expect to pay in the range of 50 cents to 75 cents per word for your book.

Option Four: Hire a professional book ghostwriter

At this level, you can expect your writer to have written several books under their own name and ghosted. They will have one or more university degrees, in English or Communications and in perhaps also in a subject area related to your book topic.

They may have a journalism background and, if so, will be skilled interviewers with a keen commitment to meeting deadlines. They have studied their craft, have reached a high level of competency and can prove it.

Ask for samples of their writing. Consider: does what they produce sound like what you want for your book? Does the book they've written speak to you, as a reader, in the same ways you want to address readers of your book? Are they adept with language? Do they sound like someone you want to work with?

The book ghostwriter may also have recommendations from other satisfied authors, though not necessarily. Even delighted named authors are often reluctant to say anything that may reveal the secret behind how their books were created. Pro ghostwriters promise to keep the names of their authors confidential. Pros honour their promises.

Professional book ghostwriters aren't 'just' writers; they are in the business of providing well-written books to authors with a message to share.

However, for non-fiction books, a new 'standard' book length has become the most popular among readers: 15,000 to 35,000 words. This is long enough to present the depth and detailed information readers are seeking, yet short enough that they can read your book in a day or two.

If you budget between $ 1 and $ 2 per word for the writing, you can expect to be able to hire a competent and experienced book ghostwriter.

You'll likely pay on the lower end of the scale for an as-told-to book and closer to the upper end for a technical topic, where the ghostwriter has a steep learning curve before being able to write your book with authority.

Option Five: Your publisher or literary agent finds your professional book ghostwriter

Ok, we've reached the exclusive and pricey top floor of ghostwriting, the one with the spectacular view.

When a rock star or Hollywood actor pens a book of diet tips or a cookbook or their backstage and bedroom confessions, or a politician authors a book that everyone expects is destined for *The New York Times* bestseller list, the named author doesn't usually hire or pay the ghostwriter.

This is often also true for books that tell the ripped-from-the-headlines stories of victims of highly-publicized crimes or people with unusual and unique stories of survival or escape or breathtaking breakthroughs in science or similarly thrilling knowledge to reveal.

If yours is such a story, chances are major publishers are already filling up your inbox or begging you to return their calls. If so, you need a literary agent, and possibly also a lawyer (solicitor) who specializes in publishing law to help you navigate the rewarding but tricky path to publication. More than a book could be involved; there may also be foreign publishing, television or movie rights to consider.

Contracts will be involved (for specifics on contracts, see Chapter Five).

You will be offered an advance against royalties on sales of your book. Your book ghostwriter will get a percentage of this advance – sometimes split 50:50 but usually a smaller cut goes to the ghostwriter and more to the author. The amounts of money involved can be astonishing when you have a dynamite story to tell with millions of potential readers lining up to buy your book. The ghostwriter will earn six figures; your advance could be seven figures.

In my research for this chapter, I found one story of a major publisher advancing half a million dollars to a named author, an American with an international reputation. The professional ghostwriter got $125,000 of this advance, which may not sound like much compared to what the named author was paid, but the ghostwriter also reportedly negotiated for a cut of the royalties. Several years later, the book is still selling briskly, the author has earned millions from that book, the ghostwriter more than $1 million and the publisher much more than this. Everyone in that deal is smiling.

People with a dynamite story to tell or who already have a big audience may be able to choose among an A-List of ghostwriters for their book. If so, your agent or publisher will send you a stack of books penned by professional authors, any of whom you could choose to write your book. These writers could also be seasoned news reporters and columnists of city or national newspapers as well as the writers of successful books published under their own names.

A surprising number of books are published every year with big-name ghostwriters behind the named author.

The reason some A-list authors take on ghostwriting assignments is to allow them the time to write the books they want to write under their own names that, while they may be critically acclaimed, may never earn out at the level of their earnings from ghosting.

Next time you pick up that rock star bio, or confessional tale from the actor or athlete who is suddenly on all the late-night talk shows or the pop singer with a cause to promote, you can bet that a ghostwriter was involved in the telling.

It's part of the craft and the art of professional book ghostwriting to make a book truly tell the named author's story, his way or her way. Exactly as if they'd written it, up close and personal, if only they had the professional ghostwriter's time to focus on the task and clever way with words.

And that's the whole point. It IS the author's story, told his way – or her way. Just told better than they would have managed on their own.

Sticker shock

Does investing $25,000 or perhaps twice that – or more – to engage a professional ghostwriter for your book shock you?

It did for some reviewers of this book in an early draft, who asked how simply writing a book could possibly be so pricey?

After all, they told me, everyone knows how to write.

That's a bit of an exaggeration. Almost every adult who had the gift of an education can write an email, a To-Do list or a brief note or text. Most people know how to do this because they do it, probably daily.

Some may also be good at writing blog posts, articles, speeches…again, because it is part of their daily lives.

Some could be good at writing longer forms, such as case studies, reports or even book chapters; though it's unlikely unless they exercise these writing muscles frequently, if not daily.

To write a brilliant book, with little or no book writing experience has been done, but it's extremely rare. So when you hire a pro ghostwriter you are paying for their honed skills, extensive knowledge and experience.

What we are considering is what could possibly justify a bill that runs to five figures – or more – for professional writing of your book?

Let me offer you a different way of thinking about the value proposition of having your book written.

The value proposition

Let's say you've just become engaged. You decide to splash out on an engagement ring that will symbolize your love and devotion to the woman – or man – of your dreams.

Jewellers advise that a reasonable amount to invest for such an important purchase is equal to about three months' salary, before deductions. If you gross $10K per month, that's a $30K token of your love that your intended will wear for the rest of your lives together.

Now let's consider another example. You need a car and your choice is new, not used. A new family sedan will set you back in the neighbourhood of $35K, before taxes and extras.

Let's compare this to another big-ticket purchase: the services of your professional book ghostwriter. Say this also comes in at around $35,000 for the book you have in mind.

The ring is a symbol of your love. If that love fails to endure, it could be that the ring is returned and you decide to sell it. You are unlikely to get more than you originally paid for it. You might – but investment wasn't the point of this purchase.

The car is a sensible expense, not an investment. You need reliable transportation, keeping you and your family safe and getting you where you need to go in comfort and style. But the minute you drive it off the lot, not only does that new car depreciate, it starts costing you money in gas, parking fees, insurance, maintenance and repairs.

Your book is different. It generates value in return for your investment, because it will make you and your services more valuable to your employers or in the marketplace (important when it comes to salary and bonus reviews or attracting a better offer elsewhere).

If you are a speaker, coach or trainer, a book helps attract new clients and is also a product to sell to these clients or at the back of the room.

If you are an entrepreneur, a book can serve as a lead generator.

If you want to extend your network, your book is a much more eloquent business card.

Smartly deployed, a quality book could double your earnings the year it is published…and continue to boost your earnings for years to come in many ways.

Additionally, the cost of creating the book is almost always deductible from your business or personal income tax, because it is a tool you use to attract new business and advance your relationships with current clients.

From a purely financial viewpoint, of these three possible purchases: engagement ring, new car, professionally ghostwritten book, the book is the one that provides your best return on investment.

You buy the ring for emotional reasons. You buy the car for reliable transportation and safety, and perhaps also for status.

You buy the book writing as an investment in your career growth and future earnings, as well as for status. It will serve as a self-promotion tool that is uniquely your own.

Professional ghostwriting, like any other service on a high level, doesn't come cheap. But it can be a valid and completely justified expense to get your brand 'out there.' As such, it could return exponentially more than what it cost to get it written, published and into the hands of readers.

What does the ghostwriter ticket price include?

The costs I've quoted include consulting between author and writer and the actual writing, usually with two revisions or as many revisions as are required.

Rarely does a manuscript need more than two rounds of revision, when there were clear expectations from the beginning and it's written by a pro.

You can expect that some revision will be required. It is a fact universally acknowledged by professional writers that books aren't written, they're re-written. Books grow organically, from concept, through research, to writing and then the re-writing/polishing to completed product.

Books always get better in the editing process. This, as any literary agent or publisher will tell you, is when the real magic happens.

The fee paid to the book ghostwriter doesn't usually include research, such as interviewing sources for the book (in a biography, for example, this would be interviews of family members, friends and colleagues).

When additional research is needed, some ghostwriters hire a professional researcher, passing the charges along to the author.

Other ghostwriters will do the research that is needed, adding a fee that is usually an hourly amount.

$45 to $100-plus per hour for research is standard, depending on the complexity of the topic.

What are the actual price ranges for professional ghostwriting? It also depends on your book's length...

It used to be that a professional hardcover book was about 55,000 to 75,000 words. This would result in a published book of 200 to 300 pages or so.

Publishers liked this length (and still do) because they could get it printed economically and sell these books at a reasonable profit margin. Readers liked this length because it had the length and heft of a 'real' book. In paperback, a book of this length fits in a larger pocket, carry-on or tote.

Anything longer would be a big book, with a price that might appeal to fewer readers (except in a few categories, such as historic romance, where readers feel cheated unless they get big books with LONG stories).

Anything shorter than 50,000 words was likely a children's book, a book of verse or recipes or one of those impulse-purchase-at-the-cash-register books.

Relatively few 'short' books of less than 35,000 words were published, except by small, specialist publishers, unless they were guidebooks.

Then came the invention of electronic books, or e-books. At the same time, there were economic downturns, job losses and wage stagnation. Suddenly, readers wanted cheaper books. Many readers were no longer willing to pay hardcover prices. Many preferred shorter books that were quick reads helping them tackle specific problems. The length wasn't what was critical to these readers. What they needed was a fast, simple, practical solution to their problem or way to improve their lives, right now, with topics such as:

- How to buy their first house, or
- Save for retirement, or
- Quit their job and travel the world.

Or:

- Start a home-based business.
- Lead by example.
- Overcome procrastination or other habits.
- Talk to their child about difficult topics, such as cyberbullying.

Or any of thousands of other practical and immediate problem-solving topics.

The shortest of these books are 10,000 to 12,000 words, a fast read that most readers will complete in one sitting. At this length, an e-book reads more like a long magazine article, rather than a book, but it usually costs the reader a lower price than either – under $ 5 (£ 4) is typical.

Readers have embraced these shorter books because they deliver value and immediate help. If you find a good one, you look for what else the author has produced and buy it. If you get a dud, at least the book didn't cost much.

Something you will want to consider is this: Will a shorter length along with a narrower or more tightly-focused book topic work best for you? Or does your topic and information require the longer length?

What would your readers prefer?

Sometimes, it is better to put out a series of shorter books, each focussing on a different aspect of a problem or situation. Or reader demographic.

Other topics can only be covered in a longer book.

While 10,000 words might sound like a lot, it actually isn't that much for a reader. You've already read more than that many words in this book, for example (total length of this book is 42,000 words).

Another length that has become popular in this century is the book that is about 20,000 to 35,000 words, or about 100 to 150 pages of a printed book. It could be that you don't really need to 'stretch out' to the longer length of 55,000 words, but can be more concise in a shorter book at about half that length. If so, you could save money on the ghostwriting.

Here is a summary of book lengths:

A short e-book, 10,000 to 12,000 words.

An e-book or print book, 20,000 to 35,000 words.

Standard length book, 45,000 to 65,000 words.

Longer book, 75,000 words-plus.

Professional ghostwriting service fees, usually paid in installments over the course of the writing would be negotiated with your prospective ghostwriter.

More complex topics and more experienced ghostwriters usually command the higher fees.

What length should your book be?

This is something you don't need to decide right now, but you will need to have some idea of length when you start talking to your book writer.

Let your topic and what your readers want to know about it guide you in deciding about the length of your book. Your ghostwriter and literary agent and publisher (if you have them) will also recommend book length.

Readers are seeking and paying for information and insights. When reading fiction, they might feel cheated by a book they think is too short, but when they read non-fiction length doesn't matter as much to most readers if they believe they are getting great value for their reading time and book-buying dollar.

Each length offers advantages, but also certain limitations

Advantages of the shorter length are lower cost to create, sell and deliver into the hands of readers. But short could also potentially frustrate readers who feel they did not get enough value, or all their questions answered or that you merely skimmed over the surface of the topic. They may protest that they need a book, but got something more like a report or extended pamphlet or long article.

Readers who feel cheated is something you don't want to experience.

A longer book costs more to produce, so must sell at a higher price. A decade and more ago, many people were happy to pay $ 35 to $ 50 for a hardcover book, but these books are a harder sell today except for authors at the very top of the popular authors lists, such as Stephen King, writer of horror novels.

The 'long read' in non-fiction is falling out of favour, with just a few exceptions such as in these topics: history; military history, biography and textbooks.

So now, let's talk some more about your topic. What will your book be about? How should you choose your subject and shape it into a cohesive whole? That's next.

Today you are you, that is truer than true.
There is no one alive who is youer than you.

-   Dr. Seuss, Theodore Seuss Geissel, in
    Happy Birthday To You, published in 1959

FOUR | What Will Your Book Be About?

Marketing students learn that people care about only three topics. These are health, wealth and relationships.

Marketers also know you can sell any quality product or service to willing (properly targeted) buyers when you are using well-crafted appeals filtered through one, or more, of this golden trio.

Say you're watching TV tonight and an ad comes on for a car. This car is like several competitors' offerings in the features and benefits. The ad doesn't talk about these benefits.

Instead, it shows a young family in the car, getting home despite logs falling on the highway and dodging an avalanche and a tornado.

Not your typical school run, but the ad makes the point that this car has superior maneuverability. It grips the road. As this car's owner, you'll be ready for anything. The appeal is to health (safety) and relationships (protecting your kids).

Clearly, this isn't going to interest teenagers who want to buy their first, fast car. Or retirees, who want maneuverability but prize reliability above everything else. While the car might appeal to them; the ad doesn't. Family buyers are who this car company is pitching to.

And now a cereal ad comes on. It promises that your kids will love that sugary cereal (No more arguments at the breakfast table!). And the secret is you're a good parent to give them this for breakfast because they're getting all these vitamins and minerals to make bones stronger. Health and relationships.

Now we get an ad for one of the Big Five banks. If you use their banking services, you'll be astonished to discover you're richer than you thought you were. Doesn't everyone enjoy surprises like this? A clear appeal to wealth.

Once you're aware of the golden trio – health, wealth and relationships - you'll spot them everywhere, including in the thousands of marketing messages we are each bombarded with every day.

Not too surprisingly, our brains are wired for survival and self-interest, and always have been since we first stepped down from the trees.

So, you may read a story about anything and find yourself thinking: how does this affect me? By which you mean: will it make me healthier, wealthier, more loveable and admired, better capable of caring for loved ones? Able to run away from bad stuff faster?

Probably this isn't a conscious thought...likely not. Why would it be? We all have brains that work this way. It doesn't need to be closely examined.

These three are the dominant survival mechanisms of our lives, simply as internalized and as automatic as the steps you go through to take your morning shower. Or brush your teeth. (Both of which actions you do because they directly affect your health, wealth and relationships). These are the habits of thinking that help humans survive.

You might choose to write a book about thermodynamics. Or how we could live on Mars. Or why robots are going to have all the jobs by 2050. Or why we must save the lions of Kenya from extinction. But unless you can tell your reader directly why he or she should care and care deeply – meaning why your topic directly, personally and importantly affects their health, wealth, or relationships -- you aren't going to have many readers.

And those you do have might not bother to read all of your ad, article or book. An un-read book is about as pointless as flying to Paris, turning around in the terminal and flying home (If Paris is home for you make that London. Or New York.)

With a bit of careful thought at the beginning, that dire fate of being pathetically, pointlessly un-read need not be in the crystal ball for you. In this chapter, we're going to discuss everything you can do to make sure your book topic is strong, meaningful and moving.

Compelling.

Simply irresistible.

An author who mastered his topic...

Napoleon was articulate, thoughtful and supremely well-read. He is said to have taken 800 books with him when he went to fight at Waterloo.

So later in life, during his forced exiles to Elba and then St

Helena, he might have written a book about Parisian urban renewal and his plans for making Paris the most beautiful city in the world, a topic he cared deeply about.

Or a saucy kiss-and-tell about the many women in his life. That could have been a fun read.

Or a less-than-flattering biography of Field Marshal Arthur Wellesley, Duke of Wellington. Another diverting topic.

Or a history of the French Revolution and its effect on France, Europe and nations beyond, such as America.

Or a discourse on the long and troubled history of the love/loathing relationship between France and England.

While he had plenty he could have said on any of these topics, the one he chose was far more personal, revealing and compelling. His ghosted book, **Memoirs**, is about the battles he fought and won, or lost, and his reasons, insights (and sometimes, excuses) about how and why these were either triumphs or defeats.

He gives us brilliance, the peaks of triumph, the horrors of defeat – and a lot to ponder.

An author in search of a topic...

Sent to interview Donald Trump for a *Playboy* article in 1985, journalist Tony Schwartz hit a wall of resistance from his subject. As Schwartz told writer Jane Mayer for her *New Yorker* article in 2016, Trump "mysteriously wouldn't answer my questions." [19] The reason? Trump told Schwartz he wanted to write a book and needed to save his best material.

---

[19] *Jane Mayer, op cit.*

Here's how Mayer reported what happened next:

What would this book be about, Swartz asked?

"My biography," Trump replied.

Swartz recalls laughing at this. Trump was only 38 years old; too young for that topic. He hadn't achieved enough yet and was then virtually unknown beyond New York's city limits.

"Yeah," Trump said. "I know."

"If I were you," Schwartz said, "I'd write a book called **The Art Of The Deal.** That's something people would be interested in."

"You're right," Trump replied. "Do you want to write it?"

And that's how Schwartz's Big Idea became the book that started the Trump snowball rolling.

Why you need a Big Idea

As author and marketing thought-leader Seth Godin says, in this century, not standing out is the same as being invisible.

To stand out, you need a Big Idea.

Here's a small idea: how to buy an exchange-traded fund online without the help and fees of a broker. This idea could be developed into a useful, interesting article for a newspaper, magazine or perhaps as a blog post.

This idea is bigger: how investing in exchange-traded funds instead of stocks or bonds could allow you to retire more comfortably and sooner. This could be the subject of a longer, more in-depth and more helpful article or a report, but this idea is a bit thin for a book.

Here's the Big Idea: how any sensible and motivated person can become a millionaire in less than five years by investing cleverly and strategically in exchange-traded funds, starting with just $1,000 and how this strategy works in any economic climate. (I doubt this is possible. But if someone came up with a way that it IS, you can be sure it'd be a bestseller.)

Note that it makes your big idea even bigger to make it more specific and more measurable.

Ok, here's another example:

Small: why some people choose to write books.

Bigger: three ways to write your non-fiction book

Big: The fastest and most efficient way any professional or entrepreneur can become the author of a professionally-written book, even if they have no time and aren't a skilled book writer. [The Big Idea behind this book.]

As you can see, the bigger the idea, the bigger the promise to readers.

The small idea might make for a column in a newspaper. Perhaps you would glance at it. But the only idea among these three that is both targeted enough and big enough for a book is the sure-fire plan to become a millionaire or become a published author of a quality book and the way to do it, step-by-step.

We could make this Big Idea even bigger with tighter targeting. Such as: how you can become a millionaire before age 30, even with student debt, even in this economy. Or how financial planners can write a book and use it to double their business in the next 18 months.

Quantifying, like targeting, makes any idea brighter and bigger.

Big Ideas usually aren't original ideas. They are often a fresh take on an 'old' idea that will help a lot of people now.

Making a million dollars (or however you define the threshold of wealth) is an old idea. But it's perennially of interest to a lot of people, especially in challenging times – that's the spin you put on this Big Idea to make it important right now.

Anyone could become rich. This isn't a Big Idea because it isn't specific enough. So, focus on a specific group of nervous investors – my choice would be young adults. That's what makes this idea new; even millennials can, with effort, become wealthy.

They may not be able to get a foot on even the lowest rung of the career ladder.

They might feel stuck in McJobs or the 'gig' economy.

They may see financial security as an impossible dream. Show them this isn't so and you've got a winner of a Big Idea.

And that's exactly what a big enough Big Idea does for you. It rises above all the white noise of life in the distracting and distracted 21st century. It promises something BIG to a specific group of hungry readers who want the refreshing combination of focus, hope and practical how-to. Really big ideas deliver inspiring results you can quantify.

A big enough Big Idea doesn't just invite attention; it demands to be noticed.

Your book makes a Big Promise, then over-delivers value to readers

Your book must reach out and grab your reader, pulling him or her into your book like a vortex, making it futile to resist.

And that's what you want – readers who simply MUST open your book and find out what you've got for them. And then stay up way past lights-out to read every word and finally reach the last page, wishing there was more.

When people hear a Big Idea, they don't say, "Gee. That's weird." They say, "Oh, right. Of course. Why didn't I think of that...?" and you've been rewarded with your first "Yes" in this new conversation. As any good salesperson knows you want to keep them saying "Yes."

That's what a good book does – it makes that reader nod their head in agreement. They are interested. Then they read a review, see the title and cover, recognize the Big Promise. Click the buy button or go find the book in a store, sit down, open that book, start to read. Keep reading, forget about everything else they 'should' be doing because they are immersed in your book all the way to The End. When this happens:

They've exited their own lives; they're living your book.

Which, for an author and any writer, is arriving in Nirvana.

Finally, closing that book with a sigh of satisfaction, they decide they have to read your next book or sign up for your speaking engagement or course, buy your product, or whatever other action you lead your reader to take right now.

Who are your readers?

I don't mean their genders, job titles, annual salaries, ages, marital status or tastes in YouTube viewing (though possibly knowing some of these demographics would be enlightening).

It isn't enough to say they're "people who like classic jazz," or "people who care about being healthy" or even "American men beyond age 50 who like to read about military leaders and battles of the ancient world."

Even though that last one is more specific, it still isn't clear enough about who your readers are.

Who are they on a deeper level, intellectually, psychologically, physically and spiritually? Do you know? It is not until you do know about your readers, beyond such superficialities as age or online viewing habits, that you get to the best hunting ground for Big Ideas.

From the first sentence of your book not only do you need to enter the head of your reader. You must join him or her in a conversation that is already going on in their head.

Your Big Idea must match your brand. Say pop super-diva Adele wants to write a book about reaching the top while staying true to herself and not conforming to the pop music stereotypes such as body-shaming.

I can imagine a lot of people would want to read that book, even beyond her legions of besotted fans. It's a hot topic she frequently speaks about with passion.

Passion – for a cause, an idea, a mission or a brand is always a magnet for the interest and attention of readers.

Though I have never had even the slightest ambition to sing anywhere except when driving alone (after that one disastrous appearance onstage, but that's another story for another book), I'd search out, buy and read that Adele book – wouldn't you?

Who doesn't want to know how to make it in a creative field, or any competitive field, while remaining true to who you are? Or what it's really like to be living a life of talent, fame and glory? These are timeless and universal themes and so a gynormous Big Idea unwraps the value in the Adele brand, contributes to it and broadcasts it. A winner all-round!

Here are more ways to come up with your passionate Big Idea:

1. Sometimes, the intersection of two medium-sized ideas gives you something that is much more than the sum of its parts, a fresh and new Supersized Big Idea.

    One that I have noticed trending lately is this: in cities with few infill or serviced building lots left, why not build mini-homes in the yards or gardens behind existing homes, entered off laneways (alleys) behind those homes in older neighbourhoods? This keeps your downtown alive, reduces pressure on commuter infrastructure and increases the tax base of downtown dwellers.

    Creating livable city homes in this way is a fresh, Big Idea in urban planning and for families who need affordable housing.

    I challenge you: what two 'ordinary' or traditional ideas in your industry or topic area could combine to be a dynamite new Big Idea?

2. If you don't already, have a listen to some TED talks.
    You'll find them at www.ted.com

    They're free to view and every single one of these short
    talks has a Big Idea as its beating heart. Inspiring!

3. What one thing is missing in your life? Think about
    it...and about if, quite possibly, other people (your
    potential readers) could feel the same? Where there is a
    Big Need (or Big Problem, or Big Pain) there is almost
    always a Big Idea to hit the spot and provide relief.

4. What one thing do you hope to have accomplished
    during your lifetime? No, this isn't your Bucket List –
    this is your prime accomplishment. Your legacy. What
    is the Big Idea there? Is this something other people are
    also striving for? What stands in their (your) way?

5. What is the most shocking, surprising, amazing,
    inspiring, or even troubling thing you've heard or read
    recently? Why did it have such an impact on you? Did
    it stick in your mind, change your thinking, or your
    behaviour in any way? Clearly it has resonance for you
    – is this also true for your potential readers?

    Here's one I noticed in a newspaper article today: it
    might be better to design smart roads, rather than
    smart cars. So what about smart sidewalks as well?
    Would these prevent accidents; save lives? How would
    they work? Can we, as a society, afford smart roads
    and smart sidewalks?

    Now there's a Big Idea that is book-sized.

6. Contrarian Big Ideas can also work. When everyone is beginning to accept a new thing as the 'best' thing, you fight the corner of the opposite or unpopular alternative. Why uni-gender schools are better learning environments for children in the primary grades is an example.

   To make it a Big Idea, you might go with something like: To Give Our Girls A Better Chance In Life, Get Boys Out Of The Classroom! There is solid science to support this idea, as there is to support educating boys in same-gender classrooms. Not, currently, a popular idea. Could make for a thought-provoking book of value to parents and educators.

What are your readers' pain points?

Here is another marketing concept that is very useful for book authors. Identify your readers' deepest, most profound pain points, then choose the most important one – that one thing they would trade almost anything for to possess or achieve or cure.

Pain points are big, immediate threats to health, wealth and relationships – in other words, everything that makes life worth living and could be threatened.

They are about to lose something they've worked hard to attain and would do almost anything to protect. Or they are blocked from getting their heart's desire.

Identify the biggest pain point for the readers you want and offer them the proven cure. If there is no cure, promise and deliver relief along with progress towards/hope for a cure.

Here's another clever way to know what your readers want

Find five books sold on Amazon with a topic similar to your planned book and appealing to the same type of reader. Go to the reviews for these five books. Read every review – the good, the bad, the indifferent, the cranky. This is free, current and valid information about what readers want to see in your book – and what they don't want.

The most valuable reviews are the ones where the reviewer didn't like the book. They will tell you exactly what they didn't like. Often, they will tell you what's missing. This is pure gold for the author ready to supply the book that delivers exactly what these readers said they were disappointed not to find in competitors' books.

Figure out who your readers are. Give them what they want. Don't give them what they don't want.

What is your brand?

And now for a fun little quiz. Match the product with the brand name:

1. The cola that promises you'll have a better, happier time surrounded by attractive young people who want to party if you drink their product.

2. The car that does more than any other to keep you and your family safe.

3. The big box department store that promises that the lowest price is their "law."

4. The restaurant that sells more hamburgers than anyone else.

5. The online store where you can buy books and almost anything else, worldwide.

6. The world's most romantic city.

7. The seller of premium coffee by the cup, made exactly as you like it.

The answers are Coke, Volvo, Walmart, McDonald's, Amazon, Paris (tied with Venice), Starbucks. These brands have spent billions of dollars to ensure that we know, like and trust their brands and become serial buyers of their products.

You won't be spending anything near their budgets to market your brand, but you will need to have as clear a definition of your brand as these world-class brands have developed.

Brand, said king of advertising David Ogilvy [20] , is the personalities of products. Branding will "make or break them in the marketplace."

Brand is quality. Brand is reputation. Brand is also destiny.

Weak brands vanish; strong brands endure.

A brand is a real promise you truthfully deliver on

Brand identity is specific.

You may describe yourself using a dozen or more adjectives, but your brand can't be a list.

It must be specific, directed to filling a major, important need

---

[20] *David Ogilvy, Ogilvy on Advertising, New York: Vintage Books, 1985, page 14.*

or desire for a specific group of people. This group, your chosen audience, is called a demographic or segment of users by marketers.

These are examples of demographics: young families with children. Or married retired city dwellers. Or women who recently graduated with engineering degrees.

Here's another way of thinking about brand. All cars are safe because they must conform to various laws and standards of manufacture. But if you're the buyer who puts safety at the very top of your must-have list, you will be more likely to buy the Volvo than the vintage ragtop Mustang in your favourite colour.

On the other hand, if you had a Volvo for years and want something sporty, that Mustang might be the brand that thrills.

Personal branding is the packaging of your values, goals and experience in a way that shows what unique solutions you can offer the specific group of people you want to influence.

Your book is the marketer of your brand and can also be proof that you can deliver on that brand promise.

The image of a brand is the logo. The logo is shorthand, instantly recognizable as representing all the promises and benefits to be enjoyed by users of the brand.

Consider these brand images:

1. A short, grimacing, black-haired and rather chubby man in a tricorn hat.

2. The Eiffel Tower.

3. A double-decker red bus.

4. A huge stature of a Grecian lady, holding up a torch.

5. Five interconnected coloured circles.

They are, unmistakably, the images of these brands: Napoleon, Paris, London, New York, The Olympics.

Many other men wore similar clothing in the late 18th and early 19th centuries, there are other Greek statues of draped females and other metal towers in the world, lots of cities have double-decker buses including red ones and anyone can draw five coloured circles, even those with zero art talent.

Doesn't matter. These symbols are sign language bonded to their brands. We've been taught to recognize the images of each of these iconic brands. They don't try to be all things to all people. They know who and what they are. They stay the course, delivering a well-known, recognized, consistent and branded experience.

And so, in your branding, should you.

Your challenge is to know your brand -- who and what you do, for whom, how and why. Perhaps you will also choose an image for your brand. Logos can be useful, but they aren't required. Your name can be the image of your brand.

Here are some questions that can help you define your personal brand from branding expert Susan Chritton [21] :

1. What keywords describe your essential qualities? Pick the three or four that are most important to you.

---

[21] *Susan Chritton, Personal Branding For Dummies, 2nd Edition, For Dummies Books, Wiley, 2014.*

2. Fill in the blank: "I know I am in my element when
   _____."

3. What is your authority factor? "People recognize my
   expertise in _____."

4. What is your superstar factor? "People comment on my
   ability to _____."

Your WOW Statement

Once you know what your personal brand is, along with your
brand image if you are choosing one, you are ready to express
your unique value in a WOW statement.

A WOW statement (or elevator statement) is your answer
every time anyone asks, "So just what is it you do?" It consists
of four parts:

1. What you provide

2. Who you help or serve

3. What's different about what you do

4. Your passion and excitement about the results – why
   you care

You WOW statement could look like this:

I use my [key skill] and [key expertise] to [achieve what] [for
whom] with [result]. This is important because it helps [higher
result] for [people served].

Note that your WOW statement is in the present. A list of
your degrees, awards or other honours has no place in a
WOW statement. It isn't about bragging or one-upmanship.

It's about relationship building, starting from, "Hello."

So, imagine that you and I happen to meet at a party. You ask me what I do. I say, "um, ah, I like to write for people. I have this project writing about, well, it's about how to do books for experts, like people at the university who..." at which point you excuse yourself to go check out the buffet. And I'm betting you won't be bringing back a plate of goodies for me because you want to hear more about this book thing, will you?

OK. Let's hit the back button.

It's party time. We're introduced and you ask me what I do. I smile and hit you with my ghostwriting business WOW statement.

"I use my journalism and storytelling abilities to ghostwrite quality popular books for business leaders and experts in personal growth and career development. I use their voice to tell their experiences, share their information and tell them stories to intrigue mainstream readers. This is important because they build their brand, extend their platform and directly engage readers. I love working with people to create thoughtful, compelling and exciting books that readers value!"

"Wow!" you say, instantly forgetting how much you'd like more of those little cheesy things on the buffet. "So, tell me more about..."

And that's exactly what a WOW statement does. It starts the conversation. It makes both an emotional and intellectual impact. It draws the listener in. It promises something. It teases.

Take a moment now to write your personal brand WOW

statement. I also suggest you write a WOW statement for your book as soon as you know your book's subject and theme (or point-of-view). Both are going to come in very handy later (and not just at parties).

Authors need to talk up their books to reach readers. Now's a good time to start.

My warning to you is don't try this off the top of your head, unless you happen to be exceptional at thinking on your feet. Much better to have a nifty WOW statement memorized, rehearsed and ready to trot out anytime.

Your Elevator Speech

Being able to reel off a good elevator speech is also a useful tool. There are times when your elevator speech is a better choice than your WOW statement. They both aim to do the same thing, just in a different way.

An elevator speech is problem-to-solution. It can be much shorter than a WOW statement, often an advantage when you have just seconds to spark your listener's interest.

1. State a problem as a "You know when x happens..." question.

2. Provide your solution

3. Tell why this matters

Here's my own ghostwriting elevator speech:

You know when a CEO needs to generate buzz and influence a wider audience, but doesn't know how to do it? I help by ghostwriting an informative, interesting book telling their stories in their own authentic voice to grab readers' attention.

Not only does this put the CEO and their company on the national radar of business leaders, it can even raise the stock price of their company!

OK, your turn. Fill in the blanks:

You know when _____?

I help them by _____.

[One or two big and thrilling benefits as a result] _____.

Your book's Mission Statement

Every business must have a vision, a mission and a strategy. Without it, no one has a clue about who you are or why you exist, including you and your colleagues.

The vision is the result your efforts attain for your company, for your staff, but most importantly for your customers.

The mission answers the question: "What and Who for?" Or "Who cares?"

The strategy is how you accomplish the vision.

You'll notice that the vision (completed books) and the mission (help people) are there in the WOW statement; the strategy usually isn't.

For your book, the vision is: Create a quality book.

The strategy and tactics? That's the topic of this book.

The mission is the one you need to answer (possibly with input from your ghostwriter): exactly what your book will deliver, to exactly whom?

Is this the right book at the right time?

It could be that you have more than one book in mind; many people do. Ask yourself, "Am I writing these books in the right order?"

Is this book timely for any reason? Is it linked to an event, series of events or the major anniversary of either? Examples of big anniversaries coming up soon are the centenaries of the later battles and end of World War 1 and of the Russian Revolution.

Is your book topic anticipating the crest of a rising trend in culture or the marketplace?

Are you in danger of writing a book that is too far ahead of the crest of interest? Or it's already too late, because that wave has already broken onshore and your readers are scanning the horizon for the next big one?

Timing matters.

Are you the best or only person who can author this book?

Exclusivity is a powerful benefit. Are you the best person to be offering this information or advice and telling these stories?

Is this book your authentic self, talking sincerely to your audience in an unique way?

Can you deliver massive value to your readers – well beyond what you promise them?

Do you have a passionate need to share what you have to say?

It won't matter if others, even many others, might have written a similar book on a similar subject. Your book will be unique because no one else has your exact combination of life experiences, skills, knowledge and insights. No one else can speak in your voice.

And it will make readers care about your topic if you care about it deeply, sincerely, completely.

A note on authenticity...who do you think you are?

Does authenticity have a bad rap in our era? Is authenticity an indulgence at best; but more likely a weakness? The butt of bad jokes on late-night TV? The reason sore-loser reality TV contestants are tossed off the island?

I believe the opposite is true. In an era of some bankers who cheat, some politicians who mislead (or simply ignore inconvenient truths) and some pop singers who can't even lip-sync convincingly, inauthenticity abounds.

But I believe as a species we have a hunger in this century for the real, the true, the genuine. My prediction is that:

Authenticity is on a roll. The inauthentic in their legions merely serve to highlight this.

We want to read your true self, not your grandiose visions of an invented self. As humans, I believe in this century we long for authentic connective-ness.

Some products and some people still use branding as protective armour; or at least as matte foundation and heavy eyeliner. I think authentic branding will become a movement in coming years; now's the time (if you haven't already) to define your authentic brand.

Get ready to meet your ghostwriter

Everything we've considered in this chapter about who you are and what your book will deliver, for what readers, is information your ghostwriter will need. If you don't have your branding, image, mission, vision, strategy and WOW statement worked out yet, the process of creating the book will develop them. You'll also need these soon to start marketing your book.

But you don't need them right away to get the ball rolling. What you do need is what we're going to talk about next.

Start by doing what's necessary; then do what's possible; and suddenly you are doing the impossible.

- St. Francis of Assisi

FIVE | Where To Start

"Begin at the beginning," the King said, very gravely, "and go on till you come to the end. Then stop."

This bit of dubious advice about how to tell a story wasn't much use to Alice. It isn't the way books are written, either, or at least none I know of (no doubt another of Lewis Carroll's sly writer jokes in **Alice In Wonderland**).

Even when the topic is chronological, such as a life story, the process is never nose to tail or bonnet to boot.

Books aren't so much written as layered on, like oil portraits or landscapes.

Books evolve between conception and completion. Usually, the last bit to be written is the opening, because it is only then that you truly know what it is you're introducing.

To an outsider looking over a writer's shoulder, the process could look chaotic and even arbitrary. It is, in fact, a process that is part craft, part art and just a dash of voodoo including the wordsmithing.

Having a process, committing to it and trusting it is the only way to prevent getting lost in the dense undergrowth of a book, or any other major undertaking.

From the midst of that project, it can be difficult to get your geographic co-ordinates, unless you know the territory because you've been this way before.

What you need before you start is some idea of what this book is going to be about, who you are writing it for and why you are writing it now. You won't necessarily know this yet. Donald Trump didn't when Tony Schwartz gave him the gift of a title and theme for **The Art Of The Deal**. Often professional book ghostwriters help their authors define a book's topic – that's Phase One of the plan.

In Chapter Two, I gave you a checklist for things you need to know, or at least have some idea about, before you engage your ghostwriter. This list is also in the **Get Your Book Written Workbook**.

Next, assuming you have found the writer you want, he or she has agreed to terms verbally and you have some – perhaps most – of the basics answered:

- My personal brand and professional brand
- Book topic
- Book theme
- Book title and sub-title
- Book approximate length
- Big Idea that makes a Big Promise to readers
- Who readers are

As we talked about in Chapter Four, the next step is formalizing the arrangement with a contract. Some writers prefer to call this a Letter of Agreement, which is a simplified contract.

Like any valid contract, it sets out the rules and it is binding to everyone who signs.

If you are working with a publisher, they will likely have a contract with you and a separate contract with the ghostwriter.

You need a plan

It's helpful to work out a book plan that goes with the contract. This plan has the specifics of what will be delivered, deadlines for each stage, amounts to be paid and when. This can be in bullet form.

Like the contract, both you and your ghostwriter need to work out, agree to and sign the Plan of Work.

You need a contract

Book Contracts from major publishers can be long and daunting documents, even thicker and more tedious to read than mortgage papers. Reading these is like hacking your way through a thicket of thorns.

If you are working with a publisher, I recommend you consult a lawyer (attorney, solicitor or advocate) who specializes in copyright and publishing law (and is intimately acquainted with those thorns) before signing. You need to be sure you understand every word. You also need advice about what is reasonable, and what is just outrageous and needs to be negotiated.

If you don't have a publisher or plan to self-publish, your ghostwriter will have a standard contract they use which is, typically, much more straight-forward. It covers what services they will provide. You might still want to have your legal advisor give it a look.

Don't cut corners by skipping a contract that you sign with the input of professional legal advice. You wouldn't purchase a house or new car that way; purchasing the ghostwriting of your book is an equally important agreement.

Here are the clauses that are usually included in a contract between author and ghostwriter:

1. **Libel Indemnity** – who is responsible for any mistakes in facts or quotes? Usually, the author is solely responsible for the accuracy of content and the ghostwriter is indemnified against libel and any other claim regarding supplied material, including copyright infringement. This clause is also specific about interviews and other materials the author supplies to the writer – what can be quoted directly? What is only for background (what journalists call "off the record")?

2. **Confidentiality** – The ghostwriter stays in the background, unless it is an As Told To book with shared credit on the cover and title page. The author does any interviews or guest appearances. The author may, or may not, acknowledge the ghostwriter in the book and elsewhere. If the book is to be credited to the ghostwriter in any way, it is usually stated in the Contract.

3. **Outline of work** – Description, including approximate book length in number of words. Specifically, who will do the work? It should be the named ghostwriter, not someone your ghostwriter subs the work out to.

4. **Deadlines** – What will be delivered to the author and when with turnaround times specified.

5. **What's included and what's not included** -- A Table of Contents and (if needed) footnotes are usually included; an Index and Bibliography are additional work, as is your Author Bio and (usually) professional editing. You, as author, are responsible for writing the Foreword or Preface or getting an authority figure to write it and for obtaining permissions for any quoted material, charts, illustrations or photos in the book. If these are included, your ghostwriter may write the captions for these, or this might be up to you.

   Getting an agent to represent the book to publishers or getting a publisher for the book is usually not included in the ghostwriting fee.

6. **Revisions** – Some writers will revise until the author accepts the work unless there is a major change in scope or direction. In this case, an hourly fee for the new writing may apply.

7. **Author Approvals Process** – What approval is and when it happens. Some authors only want to see the final manuscript from their ghostwriter; most want to see their book chapter-by-chapter or in sections. You'll sign off on approvals and any changes you ask the ghostwriter to make after that are usually additional charges.

8. **Expenses** – How ghostwriter travel and other expenses will be handled. How unusual or unanticipated expenses will be dealt with.

9. **Payment** – Total fee and fee payment schedule. Usually, a percentage to start the work and amounts at

defined stages of the writing and work delivery. For example, here is one payment model ghostwriters use: 15 percent of the total fee is due when you sign the contract, 10 percent when you approve the book outline, 25 percent when you receive the first draft of one chapter (not necessarily the first chapter), 25 percent when you receive the first draft of the entire manuscript and the final 25 percent when you get the revised manuscript.

10. **Rights and Royalties** – Copyright belongs to the ghostwriter until assigned to the author, usually after final approval and payment of the final fee installment. Copyright may be solely in the author's name or jointly held by you and your ghostwriter. Royalties due to the ghostwriter (ghostwriters receiving royalties is negotiable). Movie, TV and foreign rights, if the ghostwriter will earn a percentage on those (also negotiable).

11. **Exit Clause** – What happens if it all goes sideways? Will there be a mediation process? Usually, if the relationship is broken, the ghostwriter keeps all payments made to date and the author is free to take the writing completed to another writer to finish the book. The previous ghostwriter returns all notes, interview recordings and material related to your book. Breaking up is hard to do. Best to spell it all out in the contract.

What does your writer need from you?

1. **Access** -- The opportunity to get to know you, how you express yourself and what matters to you. This can take longer than busy authors want, but writers need this access. We spin straw into gold. Not air.

2. **Enthusiasm for this book** – Commitment to this book as an important project.

3. **Background Material** – Lots of it, including copies of articles you've written or about you or your company, information about your company or cause, notes, ideas, transcripts or recordings of speeches you've given, lists of possible sources and how to contact them and examples of writing you like.

4. **Honesty** and **Integrity.**

5. **Reasonable Patience.**

6. **Prompt return of messages** – And other professional courtesies.

7. **Prompt approvals** – If needed, concise and specific feedback if changes are needed.

8. **Prompt payment.**

The contract may also include specifics about the tone, writing style, theme and any side-bar or bonus content the writer will also provide, such as check-lists or chapter summaries.

What should you expect from your writer?

1. **Access** – This may be during defined hours; most writers need an undisturbed block of time each day to get the writing done.

2. **Enthusiasm for the topic** and for this book. Commitment to see it through to the finish line – and beyond.

3. **Excellent interviewing and writing skills**. The ability to listen deeply and ask specific, open-ended questions. Digging deeper.

4. **Delivery of work to agreed deadlines**. A good work ethic.

5. **Creativity**.

6. **Honesty** and **Integrity**.

7. **Project management skills**.

8. **Research skills**, if they'll be doing additional research – or all the research.

9. **Emotional Intelligence**.

10. **Critical thinking**.

11. **They know how to tell a story**.

12. **Able to capture and skilfully mimic the voice of the author**.

13. **Professional courtesy**.

What you expect from each other

Respect. You and your ghostwriter aren't client and supplier or boss and direct report or master and mouthpiece. You are colleagues, united on a high-performance team with the shared goal of producing the manuscript for a brilliant book.

As the author, you will need to exercise patience. You may want to 'check up' frequently on progress, but if you do, be warned: ghostwriters aren't starving artists in garrets. They are in business to produce good books for their clients. Like most business owners, they don't like anyone breathing down their necks. If you've followed the suggestions in this book and chosen wisely, you won't have any reason to micromanage your book ghostwriter.

You'll need to manage your expectations, both during the book-creation process and when you are a published author. The stony truth is that all the fame and glory of bestsellerdom is as rare as purple frogs. You likely won't have the challenges and hardships of overnight fame thrust upon you after authoring your book.

Remember your reasons for wanting to author a book. Know before you start how you are going to measure its success. Realistically, you can expect a review in your local paper, and locally is a good place to start getting media attention. A review in *The New York Times* or *The Guardian* or *The Globe and Mail* or, in Australia, *The Sydney Morning Herald* isn't impossible to attain, but it's harder than getting local coverage.

This book will be more than a paperweight on your desk, more than a brag note to your Facebook friends or coffee buddies, or more than something your mum orders a carton of and hustles at her book club.

So, what will it be? Get a clear picture in your mind of this book and what it will do for you; how it will help you in your career or personal life, or both.

With that crisply focused picture of your book, now we consider the step-by-step process of the writing.

"A goal without a plan is just a wish."

-   Antoine de Saint-Exupéry, author of **The Little Prince**

SIX | What's The Timeline For Your Book?

The Art Of The Deal, the book Tony Schwartz co-wrote with and for Donald Trump back in the late 1980s, took 18 months for Schwartz to research and then another year to write.

That, today, is an almost unheard-of length of time for a ghostwriter to work on a book. Rarely is the budget generous enough to allow that much time; rarely are publishers willing to wait that long for the manuscript they've contracted for.

In contrast, this book took 22 weeks to conceive, write, edit and publish. That's good, but not a record-breaker, for a book of this length.

The ex-athlete who needed a thesis writer

Charlie Miller's thesis, almost 30,000 words long, took three months to write and another week to type up (this was before computers with printers). His ghostwriter, as arranged by Joanna McCall, was a grade 10 student, her most promising English student at the time. Though young, this writer had already published in newspapers and at the time was writing her first non-fiction book.

"I have no doubt she can do it, with my support," Joanna told a nervous and doubtful Charlie. "Trust me. Gather up everything you've done so far including your notes from meetings with your thesis advisor. I'll get the *Chicago Style Guide* for her. We'll meet with her later today and get started."

Of the several style guides out there, the Chicago is among the best-known in America and is the one required by the university Charlie attended.

Joanna was as good as her word. The thesis, on the assigned topic (factors affecting marriage breakdown) was written by the grade 10 student under the encouraging eye of her teacher and writing mentor.

The writer's challenge was to present the information in the required format and style, using academic writing but still sounding like the author had written it. Not easy for a writer of any age, but the teenage writer managed to pull it off, with only one meeting with Charlie Miller, but firm support and encouragement from Joanna McCall.

Charlie received the manuscript, double-checked all the facts, footnotes and Bibliography listings and had the final draft typed up before submitting it, as required, to his thesis advisor.

As far as I know, only three people ever knew the details of this arrangement. Two of them are now retired.

I am the third. This is a story I've never told until now.

I was that young writer, ghostwriting a book-length manuscript for the first time. Because I was also a full-time grade 10 student with a part-time job, writing in an unfamiliar voice, style and format, the writing took longer than my nervous author wanted.

How long will it take to write *your* book?

There are too many variables for anyone to give you an accurate and absolute answer to this question, but we can ballpark it by describing the goal, then using a project management tool (there are many available as apps and free online) to map stages and progress.

Before setting this up, you and your writer need to consider:

- How much research will be needed and how much is already done? Where will this research come from? If there are people to be interviewed, who are they, where are they and how accessible are they?
- Will any of the research you have already gathered or that still needs to be sourced also need to be either transcribed or translated into English? What about fact-checking?
- Do either you or your ghostwriter have previous commitments that will lengthen communications time or delivery and turnaround of work-in-progress?

If you already know what your book will be about, have all the research done and ready to ship to your writer and have crystal clear expectations, and if what you want is a shorter book, you could have it written in as little as four or five weeks.

If, on the other hand, you need help in shaping your topic, research isn't done yet and all that is definite is that you want a book that is 55,000 words or more, your writer may need eight months or longer to deliver your book manuscript.

Most book ghostwriters take on just one, or perhaps two, ghosted projects per year. Writing a book is both focused and intensive.

To avoid burn-out, I've found that it's necessary to turn to other projects, or just take a break to recharge between book assignments. There are only so many marathons you can prepare for and run in a year.

With services in high demand, professional book ghostwriters schedule project time slots, sometimes as much as a year or two in advance. To engage the writer you want, you may have to wait. Or you may find your writer of choice suddenly has an opening.

Whether the book you want is traditional length (50,000 words or longer), short (20,000 to 30,000 words) or a quick-read mini (10,000 to 15,000 words), the process for an author working with a ghostwriter is the same.

Step-by-Step Process for Your Ghostwritten Book

1. Initial Consultation

This is a conversation, by phone or perhaps on Skype, that could last anywhere from 45 minutes to an hour. It's your opportunity to get to know the writer and decide if you think they are a good fit. Are you on the same wavelength? Do they seem like the sort of person you'll enjoy working with?

This conversation is their opportunity to find out about the book you have in mind and ask questions.

Just as you will be talking to more than one writer before making your choice, be aware that professional ghostwriters usually get more offers than they have time to commit to.

Like you, they are looking for a good fit; most won't take on a topic, or an author, they don't think they can succeed with.

After getting an overview of your book request, some writers will give you a fee range; others will quote their hourly fee. You usually won't get a confirmed price at this point. Many writers like to be sure they understand the full scope of the writing project before quoting a fee. If you pay their hourly rate, they will bill for phone calls, emails and every task related to your book's creation. A project fee usually includes phone calls and other office incidentals.

If you already have a publisher for your book, both you and your ghostwriter know what the fee will be up-front, as a split of the publisher's advance. If so, the publisher pays this advance as soon as the Contract is signed.

You don't need to worry about being frank with your potential ghostwriter during this Initial Conversation. There will be a Confidentiality Clause in the Contract, but even before it's signed, pros respect the definition of the author/ghostwriter relationship. We ghostwriters don't kiss and tell; that's not how this business works.

The ghostwriter will probably record your Initial Conversation, along with every subsequent conversation or interview related to your book. These recordings and all notes and research are returned to you after you accept and sign off on the final draft of your book manuscript (or both you and your publisher accept it, if the publisher is paying the ghostwriter).

2. Proposal

Some authors want to see a written proposal before selecting the book ghostwriter they will work with and some ghostwriters always include this step, but many don't. With other books on offer, they can decline the invitation to submit a proposal and get on with their paying work.

Here is one option, when you have spoken to a ghostwriter

who does not send out proposals: Request a confirmation of what was discussed in this Initial Conversation. Unlike a Proposal, this is a request that they can complete quickly, so you should receive it the same day as your conversation. It is usually a short email, with the points discussed in bullet form. This is a fast but effective way to be sure that you agree on what your book will cover and who your book will appeal to and the writing style, tone and book length.

3. The Contract

You have chosen the ghostwriter you want to work with, the one you feel is the best fit, based on your assessment of their writing samples, track record and your initial conversation.

Now comes the exchange of signed contracts. The initial deposit is sent to your ghostwriter. (To review what's in the Contract, see Chapter Five.)

4. Research

As soon as possible, you box up and send all the completed research, any other relevant notes and titles of books you want the writer to use. Include copies of any articles that you have written or that have been written about you or your company. Don't worry about providing too much background material – more is always better.

If your ghostwriter is going to be doing interviews, send him or her a list of who these people are and how to reach them.

You will need to call or e-mail each person on the list, telling them to expect a call from your writer. If you don't want to reveal that they are your writer, you can say something like "expect a call from my research assistant who is helping with my book," and copy to your ghostwriter.

Once the contracts are exchanged, the deposit has been received along with the research (or where to get it), your ghostwriter begins work. This could involve one or more phone or Skype conversations with you.

Some authors ask that their ghostwriter interview them in person. This may be possible, but be aware of the extra costs it adds, both in expenses (airfare, hotel, restaurant meals) but also that ghostwriters charge for their travel time. It is often more efficient as well as more practical to communicate entirely by e-mail, phone and Skype.

Many ghostwriters say that, for them, meeting in person is a distraction. They learn far more, they say, by listening carefully to the voice of their author.

Having done hundreds of interviews as a journalist and writer, both in person and via phone/Skype, I tend to agree. To write a book, I usually don't learn more by meeting the named author in person unless the book is a memoir or personal story. For a how-to or fact-based book, many ghostwriters believe it is more revealing to listen closely to what you have to say and consider how you express yourself, what words and phrases you use and what is your natural voice.

5. Book Outline

Assuming the working title, topic and theme of your book have been chosen and approved and the research is complete, your ghostwriter will create the book outline.

To do this, he or she will need to have a conversation with you, either by phone or video-conferencing (Skype). Depending on what is said in this conversation, there may need to be one or two follow-up conversations. These conversations will be recorded and transcribed.

From this, and all the research so far, your writer creates the initial book outline, usually about five to ten pages long.

This shows you the skeleton of your book. Each chapter will have a working title, followed by what that chapter will cover, usually in a bulleted list.

Mini-books may have as few as five chapters; short books will have ten or so, while longer books could have twenty chapters or more.

You and your publisher, if you have one, receive, amend and sign off on the Book Outline.

6. Expanded Book Outline

This step might be skipped for a short book or mini book, but it is always helpful for a longer book.

Usually it is a much more detailed 'build-out' of the Initial Outline and is created after all the interviews and other research are completed.

It may go back and forth between you and your ghostwriter, or between you, your agent, your publisher and your ghostwriter, two or three times to add to and amend until everyone is happy with this detailed x-ray of your book.

7. Book First Draft

Some ghostwriters write the first chapter or two chapters and send it to you to be sure they're on the right track before proceeding. Others prefer to deliver the complete first draft.

This stage can take a matter of weeks, or as long as a year, but three to six months is average for a first draft.

8. Revision

Now that you see your book, your ghostwriter will ask you to change words you just wouldn't use, perhaps delete sections you don't want or that you think aren't needed and add more facts and stories.

At this stage, you can change as much – or as little – as you want to. This is also the time when you can truly put your stamp on this book and make it your own.

Some writers set a limit on revisions; most revise until you are completely satisfied with your book. Rarely does this require a complete re-write or a major overhaul.

Revision is the stage when a good book becomes a great book.

Keep in mind that any book needs some revision. However, the choice about how much, or how little, involvement you want to have with your book at the revision stage is entirely up to you.

I have seen authors make two or three word changes; others want massive changes. When these are within the scope of the book as it was defined, and not turning the manuscript into a completely different book, this is fair ball.

While no one likes to have their work criticized, professional writers see editing for exactly what it is – improving the work. We don't take it personally because improving the work is what we both want.

Your ghostwriter makes all the required changes and additions and, when you are completely satisfied, provides you with the book manuscript, usually in a word processing file delivered as an e-mail attachment, on a memory stick or both.

The book is complete when you (and your agent and publisher, if they are involved) sign off on the Book Final Draft. At this point, the final installment of the writing fee is paid to your ghostwriter. They return everything related to creating your book manuscript.

The ghostwriter's role in creating your book is complete, but your own isn't. There's still more to do before your book is published.

We'll turn the spotlight on all that this includes, whether you're working with a traditional publisher or intend to self-publish, in the next chapter.

The future of publishing is about having connections to readers and the knowledge of what those readers want.

- Seth Godin, author and marketing consultant

SEVEN | Who Will Publish Your Book? Who Will Market It to Readers?

So far, we've talked about the writing of your book. Now we turn to the publishing and marketing.

In answer to "who will publish my book?" you have three options:

1. A major traditional book publisher.

2. A smaller regional or independent publisher.

3. Self-publishing.

Each has advantages and disadvantages. In this century, you will be directly involved in marketing your book no matter which option you choose. Even a brilliant book fails if it doesn't get in front of the eyes of the right readers, so we'll consider book marketing later in this chapter.

Finding your ideal publisher

In our century, traditional book publishers are an endangered species. The reasons are many: the tremendous costs of publishing a book and distributing it to bookstores, which are also endangered; the reader migration from print to electronic books, with their much lower selling prices and therefore lower profit margins and readers who have less time but more choices for how to spend their leisure hours (or minutes).

We live in an era of distraction and short attention spans; books must WIN their readers

The good news is that more books are being published than ever before. It was an estimated three million new titles in the United States alone in 2010, according to BJ Gallagher, writing in *Huffington Post* in 2012. That's more than 15 times as many as in 2000. This doesn't count the almost three million self-published books, book reprints or print-on-demand books in 2010, and these numbers have increased yearly since then.

There are still profits in publishing books, but less is flowing to traditional publishers, who increasingly rely on big-name authors and blockbuster books to earn their money.

Major Traditional Publishers

Major publishers know that only one in five, or perhaps one in six of the books they publish will earn back the author's advance and go on to earn royalties for the author and profits for themselves.

What this means to you is unless you already have a vast platform due to celebrity (or infamy), or your book is likely to bring a tsunami of sales like the Harry Potter books did and do, you won't have a chance with the big-name publishers. Most won't even glance at a book proposal that isn't pitched by a trusted literary agent they have worked with before.

With a major traditional publisher, there is a lot of pressure to deliver a Big Book, one with massive and broad appeal.

These publishers usually take longer to publish your book. Typically, unless your book topic is extremely time-sensitive, it takes a year or more from delivery of the final manuscript draft to publication.

Big publishers often are slower to pay. They direct most of their resources to their Big Name and bestselling authors. If you are one of these, life can be rosy, though author book tours with authors being luxuriously indulged are almost unknown today. Even if you do win a contract from a traditional publisher, odds are high that you and your book will go to the purgatory of 'mid-list' authors.

If it's your intention to place your book with a big-name publisher, I recommend that you put all your efforts into getting a literary agent. Agents only take on authors and books they know will sell for a substantial advance because agents make their money on a percentage of the author's earnings.

How to find a literary agent

1. Look online and at directories you will find in city libraries for names and addresses of agents who handle books like yours.

2. Look in books you like and see if the author thanked their literary agent in the Acknowledgements.

3. Ask authors you admire who their agent is and if they can introduce you.

4. Talk about your book to friends, family, colleagues and

    acquaintances. You never know who can point you in the right direction.

Literary agents take a cut of your earnings as author. They work hard for the money, finding the best publisher for your book, negotiating the best deal for you, helping sharpen the theme and in other ways serving as a sounding-board for ideas, mediating any disagreements with your publisher or publisher's editor and much more.

If there's any chance that your book might be published abroad, made into a TV series, a movie, a graphic novel or any other transmutation, you need a literary agent to broker the deals and make sure you get paid what you're owed.

Your Book Proposal

The way you initially approach an agent or a publisher is with a book proposal. It usually consists of a cover letter, brief description of the book, sample chapter or two, a brief bio of you as an author (publishing credits, awards) and how you plan to help market the book.

The ghostwriting fee for creating your book proposal package is usually not included with the fee to ghostwrite the book.

Small, Regional and Independent Publishers

Smaller publishers tend to have much smaller budgets; often offering no advance at all.

When they agree to publish your book, they take on the work and expense of the many tasks that lie between manuscript

and finished book: editing, permissions, cover design and cover copy, book design and formatting, ordering proofs, correcting proofs, ordering the print run, re-formatting for e-book, re-formatting for different book delivery platforms, and more.

One advantage of working with a smaller publisher is you likely won't have a literary agent; you'll work with your editor and publisher directly.

Smaller publishers don't have a mid-list. They may only publish a few titles a year, so each book and every author gets their devoted attention. They're also more nimble than larger publishers, sometimes able to publish a book within weeks rather than many months after receiving the manuscript.

The Self-Publishing or Indie Option

Jane Austen self-published, as did William Shakespeare and many other authors of superb works treasured by millions of readers, but they and every other writer of earlier centuries lived and wrote in a very different publishing climate than ours. In their centuries, self-publishing was respectable.

More recently, the thinking was that if you resorted to self-publishing, your book must be so amateurish that no 'real' publisher would take you on.

Collections of recipes offered as fundraisers, most poetry, stories about beloved pets poorly told, collections of long and uninspiring sermons, family memoirs, travel memoirs...all were 'published' by what was known as vanity publishers.

 Often these publishers preyed upon their authors. What the hapless authors received for their investment was, usually, a few boxes of books. Lightly edited or not edited at all, most of

the service vanity publishers delivered to their customers was in the usually overpriced and often shoddy printing.

A few vanity publishers still exist, but today most of the authors who might have been their customers prefer true self-publishing. With some authors becoming both rich and famous without ever having a publisher – big, small or vanity – self-publishing has changed the publishing landscape.

Today, almost anyone can self-publish their e-book, though there is a learning curve to do this. Alternatively, you can hire people skilled in the various steps required to self-publish your book as an e-book and as a print book.

If you chose the self-publishing route, you'll need to do these tasks or hire them done:

1. Edit the manuscript.

2. Add in the table of Contents, copyright page and other elements if these will be included: preface or foreword, bibliography, footnotes, author bio.

3. Design the book, choosing fonts and spacing. Put in photos and their captions, side-bars, graphs and illustrations, if any.

4. Format the book to be attractive, readable and in compliance with the platform it will be sold on – Amazon, Nook, Kobo and others. You could also sell your book in other formats, such as pdf, directly from your website.

5. Develop a cover concept and get the cover created by a graphic artist.

6. Write the cover copy, if there will be a print edition of the book.

7. Arrange for ISBN number, the International Standard Binary Number that is also the barcode to sell the book. The process to apply for a book's ISBN differs according to the author's nationality. Americans buy the ISBN for their book. In Canada, your ISBN is issued by the federal government to authors at no cost. Look online for details relevant to your country. You'll need a different ISBN for each format of your book – e-book, print book softcover, print book hardcover/library binding.

8. Write the marketing copy for the book.

9. Get a professional author photo taken. This is usually a flattering head-and-shoulder shot in colour.

10. If there will be a print edition of the book, order the proof copy, make corrections, create the index (if there will be one) and any extras to the book, such as bonus materials or an accompanying workbook (which is the bonus that comes with this book).

Where do I find help? What will it cost?

Look online on work exchange sites to find skilled help.

You can expect to pay these amounts (in US dollars) for:

Research

$ 45 to $ 80-plus per hour, depending on complexity of the topic.

Professional translating

30 cents to 50 cents a word.

Interview transcribing

$ 3 to $ 5 per 250 words.

Book cover design

You can buy a cover design for as little as $ 6, or spend as much as an author I know of who was delighted with the cover she paid "only $1,200 for" she told me, "and I love it." Frankly, I thought her book's cover was good, not great, but she was delighted with it. It took a year of sales to earn back her investment in just the cover design.

Covers matter. A dreary cover can sink the sales of an otherwise excellent book.

If you are a competent photographer, you could use one of your photos for your cover. There are many places to get royalty-free photos online at no cost, but I haven't found it worth the time it takes to search their vast sites for the few gems among a lot of mediocre images.

Instead, for our self-published titles, we pay $ 8 or $ 10 or so for the use of an image from one of the stock photo agencies, such as istockphoto.com or stockfresh.com.

Then, using simple photo editing software, we alter those images, perhaps cropping them or bumping up the contrast to help make our covers unique. We hire a graphic artist to use that image to create a dynamic cover.

If you self-publish, I suggest you have two or three covers made, then survey your friends, asking them to pick the one with the most impact. You can do this for free using social media such as Facebook or a survey tool such as surveymonkey.com. People love helping authors, you quickly learn which of your covers has the most impact and you get word of mouth started about your book – triple win!

Book editing or indexing

$ 15 to $ 50 per hour, depending on the complexity of your topic. Book editing is critical. Professional writers turn in polished manuscripts, yet still fresh eyes can spot mistakes or missteps that the author and writer have missed.

You need a second and probably a third critical reader, not to make your book 'perfect,' but to eliminate anything that breaks the spell for the reader. Most readers can be charitable about one or two small mistakes, but more than that and they may toss the book aside in disgust...or simply decide to go check out what's in the fridge or glance at their emails and somehow never get back to your book.

There are three types of editing:

1. **Initial content editing** to check – does the book make sense? Are there gaps to be filled with more information, quotes, stories? Are chapters in logical order? Is there any section or chapter that needs to move somewhere else in the book, or be deleted? Does the book stay focused on topic? Is it clear and meaningful? Does the content fully deliver on the promises made in the title and first chapter? Does the content overdeliver value to the reader?

2. **Copy editing** – does the book content flow or is it choppy, in need of smoothing out? What about word choices and correct word usage? Tone and writing style?

3. **Proof-reading** – to catch any spelling, grammar or punctuation errors.

Getting in front of the eyes of your readers

No book that has ever been written sells itself. Every book requires marketing.

"Achieving publishing success is 5 percent writing a good book and 95 percent marketing," as Jack Canfield and Mark Victor Hansen, of **Chicken Soup For The Soul** said. [22]

Marketing is a vast topic, one that can fill several good books and already has. It can be overwhelming. Advice books I have read for new authors give a daunting number of steps you should take, along with often conflicting advice about what works best right now. There is a learning curve for every one of these tools.

Don't be like an author I know – a single father who decided to take a year off from his job to "be an author." Before that year, he had written a book on a trendy self-development topic, writing evenings and weekends. It was an heroic accomplishment given his other commitments. Now his book was self-published and he had just a trickle of sales, which is what happens to almost every newly-published book by an unknown author. Everything would change, he thought, if only he could devote more time to selling his book while writing his next book.

His final day at his nine-to-five was December 31. A few months later, we happened to meet and I asked how the new fulltime writing life was suiting him.

---

[22] B. J. Gallagher, *op cit.*

"To tell the truth, I haven't written anything except articles and posts for other people's websites for months," he said. He found he was spending all his time "pushing the first book."

Marketing his first book had turned into a full-time job plus overtime. He was working harder than ever – selling some books – but earning a fraction of what he had in his former job.

It easily happens when you self-publish and are desperate for sales and income. You can put yourself on a treadmill of stress and marketing misery. Better to understand what marketing is, and what it isn't. What it can and should do for you...and what is just spinning your tires on black ice, as my friend seemed to be doing.

Let's start with what marketing isn't. According to author and book marketer Tim Grahl: [23]

- Marketing isn't sleazy car salesman tactics.
- Marketing isn't tricking people into buying.
- Marketing isn't unethical.
- Marketing isn't intrusive self-promotion.

Marketing <u>is</u> two things: (1) creating lasting connections with people, through (2) a focus on being relentlessly helpful.

How to Market Your Book

Today, most book marketing is done by the books' authors.

This is true even for those published by major traditional publishers, who devote most of their resources to their A list authors who have built a large base of faithful readers.

---

[23] *https://booklaunch.com*

Even these A listers have to help market their own books and are also asked to help market their publishers' other authors, for example by providing testimonials, cover blurbs or writing reviews in high-profile publications such as *The New York Times*.

Readers seldom take the time to read a book by someone they have no connection with and have never heard of.

How do you and your book connect with readers?

Start with your own community of family, friends, co-workers and peers in your industry. Tell them what you're doing and why. Here's one place where your WOW statement will come in handy. Ask your community to read your book, review it if they like it and tell their friends. Don't be disappointed when most don't do any of these things. It's not personal; they're just busy. Persist, without being a book pest.

To do this, create these (if you don't already have them) in this order:

1. Your author website

2. LinkedIn Profile

3. Facebook Page

4. Amazon – claim your author page

5. Goodreads – claim your author page

6. A list of potential readers and fans.

As with all things computer, each of these requires learning how to use a program or a website or software. There is an abundance of how-to info out there for each of these. If you don't already know how to do your LinkedIn page or Facebook page, there are helpful tutorials on their sites and posted by users on YouTube and Vimeo.

Putting up a website is more complicated. There are e-books available telling how to do it, if you want to do it yourself. For the tech-averse there is also the option of hiring someone who knows how these things work and can walk you through it, either long-distance via Skype or Facetime, or (better) in person. Teenaged children or grandchildren tend to be very good at this sort of thing and their services usually come at an affordable price.

If you don't have any tech-savvy teens under your roof, ask around. Most of us don't have to look too far to find teens or young adults with impressive social media skills who might be talked into helping out the 'oldies' in exchange for a gift certificate to the shopping experience of their choice.

Before you are ready to post your website or social media content, you need to write it. Or hire someone to write it for you. As is true in hiring a ghostwriter, you should look for a professional website writer. Effective website writing is different in tone and style than book writing or email writing or any other writing format.

Just like your book, posts, articles and emails, your website needs to be what people want to read or you lose the opportunity for their buy-in.

Here's what your author website needs:

1. **Home Page** with a picture of the cover of your book and a link to buy it. Your WOW statement can help you create the content of your home page.

2. **About Page**. This is about you as an author – it expands on why you wrote the book. Add a flattering photo of yourself and the cover of your book.

3. **Testimonials Page** – all the nice things readers have said about your book, the more the better. At first, you won't have many, but even three is enough to start with. Send a pdf of your book to three friends, ask them to say something nice, and use these for your first testimonials.

4. **Blogs Page** – posts or articles you write to help market your book. News about where you will be speaking, teaching a course, or conferences you will be attending. Teasers about your next book. Your most recent post is always at the top of the page. Readers scroll down to see previous posts.

5. A way to **contact** you. Put this on every page of your website.

Next, establish or add to your Facebook page and LinkedIn page. Each is free, though you might want to consider the paid version of LinkedIn which offers more features.

Each is straight-forward to set up, walking you through the process. You simply type in the answers. Post your photo on both.

If you are selling your book on Amazon, and I recommend you do because it is the world's biggest bookseller, claim your author page. The process is simple. Post your photo here, too.

Send an email to everyone you know, telling them about your new book and asking them for permission to contact them from time to time with book news from you. Those who say yes are the first subscribers to your list.

At first, with just a handful of names, you can easily send out a group email whenever you have book news to share. Later, when the number of names on your list grows, there are inexpensive programs to handle your list such as AWeber, MailChimp, Get Response and Vertical Response.

Send a brief, bright email to your list subscribers a few times a month or so, no more. For every email that asks your subscribers to do something – review your book, buy your book, be a beta reader of your next book – send four messages that give them something but don't ask for anything. Make the something you give them interesting and valuable.

In writing a book I have found that there is always good material – quotes, information, ideas – that don't make it into the book. Sometimes this is because something doesn't quite fit. More often because research and interviews have produced such a bounty of good stuff it can't all be used in the book. But it is pure gold when it comes time to market your book, because what didn't make the cut can be crafted into checklists, tips sheets, blog posts and articles.

Here's how to use these:

1. Post them on your website. Send an email to your list telling them about this new content and linking to it.

2. Post them as articles on LinkedIn.

3. Post a link to them on Facebook.

4. Offer them to owners and editors of influential websites that your potential readers know, like and trust. Start with the sites you follow, then do a search for similar sites.

The most influential sites to contribute to for American writers are *Huffington Post* and *Forbes* magazine if you write about a business- or career-related topic. It takes effort to get accepted with either but is worth the effort.

You won't be offering the same post or article everywhere. Be selective about who gets what. Also, don't fall into the trap of writing reams of content you give away to other users. Always get a link back to your website for your contributed content and a mention of your book.

> *Like creating your book, marketing it is playing a long game.*

Marketing is something you need to do some of, every week. No one thing will work to get you all the book sales you want forever. Each thing you do adds to what you've already done. Some things work less well than others. What's important is to have a plan and persevere.

Results accumulate with time. To keep your marketing from swallowing you live (as it did for most of a year for the friend I told you about) I suggest you make a marketing plan for your book with do-able tasks – say one blog post or the equivalent per week and two messages to your list per month. Each quarter, do one Big Push for your book.

This doesn't sound like a lot, and it isn't. But over time, it will build momentum, without overwhelming you.

Your One Big Push this quarter could be:

1. Send a news release to local newspapers and radio stations that have talk shows. The result you hope for is being invited for an interview. If you are, have it recorded by a friend. Post it on YouTube or Vimeo and on your site. Talk it up.

2. Have a friend interview you – just asking one or two questions your readers have. Record your answers and post as an audio on your website or a video in Vimeo or YouTube that links back to your website. Or do a brief how-to video on a topic related to your book.

3. Give a speech at a local service club or trade association related to the topic of your book. Ask someone to tape it and post it on your website. Let your email list know about it and link back. Post it on Vimeo or YouTube with a link back to your site.

4. Go to a conference. Meet the top experts related to your book topic. Network. Hand out bookmarks with a photo of your book and contact details. (These can be ordered cheaply online.)

5. Find a mentor or re-connect with your mentor and ask for introductions. Tell your mentor the type of people you want to meet or connect with.

6. Join a trade or professional association related to your career and/or your book. Volunteer to a committee or two to get to know other members. Consider a small ad for your book in the association's newsletter, directory or on their website.

7. What is the one leading-edge or 'next generation' technology, strategy or knowledge-area in your field that is currently in the news – or is just about to burst on the scene? Consider it, and how you could tie it to your book's topic. Think of ways you could get readers to connect the dots between this breakthrough and your book. My suggestion is to pick ONE breakthrough. Be very specific. Then list the many ways you could present this connection between this breakthrough and your book. Your list might include:

a) give a speech on this topic – the breakthrough is exciting new information.

b) have someone record your speech and post it to YouTube or Vimeo, linking back to your website.

c) write a 'bonus' chapter for the book and distribute it free to your list or as the 'first chapter' of your next book.

d) write posts for blogs related to your topic, with a link back to the sales page on your Facebook Book Page or website (readers find a link there to buy your book).

Think about where your readers are right now. There are many ways you could influence them. Choose the two or three that are most likely to get your words in front of their faces.

8. Create a course related to your book topic. It could be a series of videos with related checklists, worksheets or assignments. Sell the course on your website.

9. Interview an expert. Post the audio or video or article you write about this interview on your website and ask the expert to also post it on his or her website. Link to it from both LinkedIn and Facebook. Tell your list about it. Invite them to share it with their friends.

10. Host a contest. Solicit prizes from friends with small businesses or websites selling products to help publicize them and their wares. Do some cross-promotion.

11. Get creative about what else you could do that's fresh, different, eye-catching. For example, does your book

topic or title lend itself to merch such as coffee mugs, tee shirts, posters or calendars? Offer these on your website – profits could double what you earn from your book and help sell more books!

12. Who could you partner with to market each other's books or products? Reach out with an email, a LinkedIn message or a proposal. Ask them if they'd like a free copy of your book. Follow up.

There is a marketing chestnut that says that the most effective sales method is word-of-mouth.

This isn't just some old nut, it's true. But you must **do** something to get those mouths to start talking and that takes time, money or both.

And once you do it, keep doing it to keep them talking. Marketing is an on-going effort, not a one-off. Think of it not as a race; not as a marathon, but as a life-giving constant, like breathing.

It is too easy to get swallowed alive by your marketing To-Do list. Avoid this by setting realistic goals for your marketing efforts. Do what you can do with the time and money you're able to devote to marketing your book. Some of these methods will sell books; some won't produce immediate results, some won't produce any results but some will also surprise you.

Keep going.

Remember that usually you can recycle what you write (or hire a writer to produce). An article or speech can be refashioned as a checklist, a post, an email to your list or a series of emails or a video topic or even all of the above.

Always be on the lookout for ways you can deliver incredible value to your readers. This may be by partnering with people who also have something to offer that your readers would love to know about (and buy)! Don't be shy about approaching anyone with a good product or service that fits with your book and you think your readers would like to know about.

Just as is true for your book, quality content is more important than quantity.

Keep putting good content out there, keep telling your potential readers about it and gaining their trust, and your book will succeed, as will you as an author and expert.

If it all begins to seem like too much of a good thing, scale back. Keep what's working, testing only one marketing method at a time and measuring the results.

Remember, you can hire help for many of these tasks. There are plenty of people offering these services online. Two places to look are fiverr.com and upwork.com.

> *As the best marketers teach us, it's all about know, then like, then trust before they buy.*

A marketing master I once studied with likens marketing to courtship. Before the first date, you need to meet. There needs to be that initial spark of interest. Sparks must to be fanned gently to leap into fire.

You don't propose on the first date. You don't move in together and set up joint accounts. You don't start checking out your school catchment area while painting the smallest bedroom white, hanging pictures of lambs and bunnies and installing a rocking chair by the window.

What you do is go for some dinner, or maybe just a drink, and you talk a bit. Gently.

If the talk is good, there could be a second date. And a third. All the while, you're getting to know each other. Getting a sense of who this person is, what matters to them, what they want in life and if they're worth your time and interest. If you'd like to see them again.

Or not.

Marketing is also a slow, courteous, kindly, consistent courtship. Possibly leading to commitment and intimacy.

Not to be rushed, because it takes two. And it takes time.

The next two chapters are about why the readers you want to court are going to like you and trust you.

And really, really want to know you better.

Good writing does not succeed or fail on the strength of its ability to persuade. It succeeds or fails on the strength of its ability to engage you, to make you think, to give you a glimpse into someone else's head.

- Malcolm Gladwell, in his introduction to **What The Dog Saw And Other Adventures**

EIGHT | What Is Good Non-fiction Writing?

Asking "What is good writing?" is like asking, "What is good art?" Or what is a good movie, novel, sonnet, concerto, or cherry cake? Unless the person answering is a professional in that form of expression – drawing, painting, acting, directing, writing or baking, how can they possibly know? Most of us simply resort to saying, "Well, I know what I like."

If you like it, it must be good, surely? And dreadful if you don't?

The problem is this likability meter is wonky. It is entirely subjective, like Simon Cowell judging fashion designers on *Project Runway* (which as far as I know he has never attempted but it might be fun to see him try) or me judging ice dancing at the Nationals.

Liking the book your ghostwriter delivers is a good thing. But it doesn't necessarily mean you've received excellent value for your book ghostwriting time and money investment.

Does the happy fact that you like your book or even love it insure that multitudes of readers will like it, too? Enough to shell out their hard-earned after-tax dollars (pounds, euro, yen) for the pleasures of reading every single word?

Alas, no.

Let's look at what you want to see in your book's manuscript. And why it matters that you and your ghost get it right.

Clarity and Strength

Clear thinking becomes clear writing. No one enjoys reading a non-fiction book that isn't clear and full of meaning.

"Good writing has an aliveness that keeps the reader reading from one paragraph to the next.... It's a question of using the English language in a way that will achieve the greatest clarity and strength," Yale University English and writing teacher and author William Zinsser says. [24]

Clear writing is toned and muscular; never flabby, whiney or wimpy.

Clear writing stands up straight, shoulders back and makes eye contact.

Clear writing offers its information and stories in a crisp, clear, straight-forward way. It remains focused on the topic and theme. It is not an information-dump that the reader must clamber through like the home of a hoarder, struggling to make sense of it all.

It is a cohesive collection of curated insights, ideas, information, quotes and stories. It has a strong voice. A specific point-of-view. A logical structure.

---

[24] *William Zinsser, On Writing Well, 30th Anniversary Edition, New York: Harper Perennial, 2016.*

Clear writing is like a good three-course meal, made with fresh ingredients. You savour each bite and leave the table satisfied. Nourished and pleasantly full; not overstuffed.

The courses of this writing meal for fiction are:

Appetizers -- We meet the people, are shown how they relate to each other and learn about the problems and challenges they face, stimulating our appetites for the next act.

Main Course – A big plate of struggle, small wins, bigger losses and set-backs, a black moment when all seems lost and hopeless. We've dined well on plot, theme, characters and their development but are left wanting something more ...

Dessert – Our reward for sticking with these characters through every bite. With one final effort, the hero breaks through the crust on our crème brûlée to the sweetness beneath, having earned a happy ending – or one with the bitter taste of tragedy.

Coffee or a Liqueur at the end is the last few loose ends tied up. We sigh with contentment as the credits roll or the cast take their bows.

This is the structure of stories, but it is also the structure of many non-fiction books. If your book is a memoir or autobiography, you are the hero facing and ultimately overcoming the problems or challenges on the journey to success. Or ultimate failure, but lessons have been learned, perhaps earning redemption.

Alternatively, it could be that the 'hero' of your story isn't a person, animal or any living thing. It may be a product, a type of service, a company, a brand, an emerging technology, a social movement or a new threat to human health, wealth or relationships that is the epic character of your story.

If so, be sure you make the connection to human survival, productivity, happiness or success very clear.

Tone & Attitude

The tone of your book may be academic, business, engineering or medical, as in medical journals. This is a more formal, stiff tone than the casual tone and attitude of non-fiction books for a popular audience.

Consider your reader, possibly tired after a long day or week at work. Or perhaps they're distracted, as all of us so often are. As a result, readers are unlikely to pick up a 'difficult' book by choice. If they do read a 'thick' book, it is for a bigger goal, such as passing a course, getting the next certification in their field, catching up with peers' research and similar reasons. If they are reading non-fiction, most would rather spend their leisure time with a book that is interesting and helpful, but conversational in tone.

They are reading for information, but also for entertainment and escape into someone else's way of thinking and world. Just as you are right now.

They want to expand their horizons, think and feel in a different way than the familiar, enrich their experience of life without leaving the comforts of home.

They want to be taken by the hand and walked down the garden path of your topic, while you, their trusted guide, point out the spectacular plants and hardscaping along the way.

Did you trip at that word, "hardscaping?" It's likely, unless you are a garden designer, landscaper or hard-core gardener. All this word means is the garden elements made of lumber, stone or metal, such as the raised beds, patio flag stones or garden benches. Walkways, driveways, outdoor kitchens and fencing are hardscaping, usually the elements that go into the garden first, before the planting.

It interrupts the flow to come across that bit of gardening jargon. Jargon, of any industry or profession, is great if you are writing exclusively for 'insiders' in your field. It might offend anyone else, one of the 'outsiders.' No one wants to feel like an outsider, especially in the intimacy of this budding relationship they're enjoying with you while reading your book. Break the flow and you lose your reader.

Casual, conversational style, written in the way you would talk to a friend, is what readers respond positively to in mainstream, popular books.

Engineers like talking to each other in engineer-speak because, within the group, it communicates effectively. Doctors have their own professional language for the same reason, as do editors, dentists, accountants, bankers, stockbrokers, electricians, architects and just about any other trade or profession (including writers).

Yet, in their few moments of leisure reading, most 'insiders' would rather not read even more in their tribal language. They get enough (likely more than enough) of that at work. When they read your book, unless it is designed specifically for an audience of your own tribe, they want something easier to read.

More enjoyable.

Requiring less of an effort on their part, because they're tired. Winding down from their day. Ready to relax, maybe learn something, find out how to get relief from a problem, while also being entertained.

By entertainment, I don't mean that your book needs to be a comedy routine. I do mean that it makes it pleasant and even easy for the reader. There is flow. Good transitions. Interesting facts. Stories that might be worth repeating at coffee time or over the dinner table.

In other words, you give your reader a smooth ride with a clear view. Just like a good newspaper or magazine article.

Completely unlike a report, a white paper, a text book or an article in a trade magazine.

Logical Structure and Order

A garden path leads to somewhere, and so should your book.

All good writing has an internal logic. Each chapter builds on the content of the ones that came before.

You sell your reader a ticket (the price of the book) to a desirable destination and then you take him there, in style and comfort.

A well-written non-fiction book is not like a collection of short stories – each able to stand on its own merits. If your book will be a collection of articles, they must be arranged and edited so there is an internal logic and the necessary overarching book theme (your Big Idea) and connective tissue.

Transitions between paragraphs, between sections of the book and between chapters are your connective tissue.

Without smooth transitions, it can be a bumpy ride for your readers. They'll be feeling queasy.

Writing in 'Newspaper Style'

Journalists who write news stories use what is called the inverted pyramid to structure their stories. The most important information goes up top, followed by explanation, followed by even more details down to the most insignificant facts or quotes at the end.

Historically, this inverted pyramid structure was a rule written in stone for news stories because a too-long story could be chopped at any point to fit and still make sense. Readers might have objected to abrupt endings; typesetters didn't. They had a paper to get out.

Today, typesetters have gone the way of the eight-track and boom boxes. Editors don't chop to fit; reporters write to fit and (mostly) edit themselves.

Feature writers, magazine article writers and non-fiction book writers use a different structure. There are plenty of structure choices a writer can make, but essentially the structure of an article or a chapter is this:

Big Hook Beginning that teases interest and entices readers to keep reading, usually with a Big Promise of what they will get if they do, directly stated or implied.

Middle that is filled with the most interesting, relevant facts and quotes, delivering on the Big Promise.

Ending that wraps it all up with a twist, a surprise, or comes full circle back to the big hook. Book chapters often end on a cliff-hanger or a promise.

In a book, not only is this the structure of each chapter, it is the overall structure of your book. What in fiction is called story arc, with rising and falling action. And plenty of suspense, to

keep your reading turning those pages.

Sentence Structure

A century ago, readers were content to amble through a sentence that reached into the next page, liberally scattered with phrases and clauses, colons and semicolons.

Not today. Both sentences and paragraphs need to be shorter and snappier to keep readers' attention.

Sentence length must vary to keep readers from dozing off. Paragraphs should be two, three or sometimes four sentences; rarely do they need to be longer.

Lists are easier to read in bullet form.

Writing Voice

Using stiff formality, lots of long words and long sentences are still considered acceptable in some business, academic and professional writing. But even in professional writing, readers have grown weary of sentences as long and heavy as an overloaded double transport (articulated lorry).

Stilted writing, long words and long sentences are the mark of an amateur writer who is trying to impress.

Readers want the precise, the crisp, the direct.

What they value is your authentic voice and your unique message, not something that could have been written by anyone. They want it to be vivid and personal.

Vivid writing uses active language.

Active sounds alive. Passive sounds tired.

The message was picked up by Sharon is passive. You want the most important element of the sentence to come first. Usually, this is the person.

Sharon picked up the message is active. Shorter. Snappier.

Vivid writing uses active verbs. (Verbs are the action words.)

Three birds are in the nest – 'to be' verbs are overused, making them sound weary. Use vivid verbs.

Three birds huddled in the nest – is more active, specific and interesting, because next we want to know why they're huddled. This active verb moves the reader further into the story.

Use of Adverbs and Adjectives

Adverbs are the words that describe verbs. Adjectives describe nouns. Such as:

The beautiful red-haired lead performer in *Poldark* is the talented, charming newcomer Eleanor Tomlinson. – The adjectives are beautiful, red-haired, lead, talented, charming, newcomer. The subject and noun in this sentence is performer.

She quickly got into the rowboat. --The adverb is quickly. Got is the weak verb. Better would be: She leapt into the rowboat.

Better would not be: She eagerly and quickly leapt into the rowboat on the pearly, storm-tossed sea. This sentence is going to sink under its own overblown weight.

Storm-tossed sea is acceptable for romantic poetry from another era, but purple prose today. Purple prose makes you sound like poor daft Aunt Tilly.

Adjectives and adverbs, used sparingly for effect, can help

paint the picture in your readers' minds. Choosing a more active, lively noun or verb is almost always the better choice.

Good writing doesn't serve up everything to the reader on a plate. It allows him or her to arrive at their own conclusions, given the way you have framed the information.

Good writing never condescends. Talk to readers as you would to a valued friend who doesn't have your background in the topic. There is both art and craft in opening a window on complex, 'difficult' topics, making them understandable for readers in a fresh way.

Humour instantly makes your reader more relaxed and more receptive to everything you'll say next. But be careful with humour, and especially with jokes that can easily backfire. What one reader finds hilarious could offend another.

If you are going to use humour, irony or absurdities are better choices than sarcasm or put-downs that leave a bitter taste. One easy and sure-fire tactic is to quote someone saying something funny that is relevant to your topic.

Positive Voice

Beware of negatives and especially double negatives.

This is a negative: He didn't arrive.

The meaning here is unclear. Maybe he was late. Or he never arrived. Possibly he never even started out? Got lost? Who knows?

Much better: He arrived after 7 p.m. because of the traffic.

Double negative: He didn't ever arrive without bringing a gift.

Much better: He always brought a gift.

Human brains are attuned to positive messages and less able to take in negative messages. We find double negatives confusing.

We are also much more capable, as a species, of solving problems than preventing them.

As much as is possible, cast your message in positive language.

Accentuate the positive.

Eliminate the negative.

And don't mess with Mr. Inbetween.

Storytelling

"In every set of lyrics, the Rolling Stones told an incredible story," Randy Bachman told his *Vinyl Tap* audience on November 20, 2016. [25]

Of course they did, those clever lads. So did and do the Beatles, Beach Boys, Norah Jones, Jim Croce, Cole Porter and every other playwright, scriptwriter, lyricist, balladeer and book writer, past and present, who touched or touches the hearts of their audiences.

Good stories, well told, earn readers.

Readers crave stories. They seek them out. They respond to stories and they share them.

---

[25] *Randy Bachman, host of Spinal Tap, broadcast November 20, 2016 on CBC Radio Two (Canadian Broadcasting Corporation) and internationally on Sirius FM.*

Why?

The theory is that story is not merely hard-wired in our brains, it is in our DNA. It is story that accounts, in large part, for the survival of our species. In story, we passed along knowledge, answering the critical and emotional question, "Will this help me or hurt me?"

- Is it safe to eat these little green berries, or are they poisonous?
- When you get up close to that polar bear and jab him in the leg with your spear, what happens? Does he fall over dead, or turn around and eat you?
- What causes this belly-ache? Is it because I didn't paint my belly with this berry juice? If I do the correct body painting in the correct patterns, will this pain go away? What stories do the elders have about this situation?

We shared vital information about how to survive through story long before anyone knew how to write stories down or carve them on walls.

Story is how humans think, Lisa Cron says in her book, **Wired For Story**. Story "is how we make sense of the otherwise overwhelming world around us." [26]

We tell stories because we need them, not merely as entertainment. Without stories, our world and all of existence is chaos, something humans have low tolerance for because it's dangerous.

Why anecdotes aren't stories

Anecdotes or events present a slice of life, but not a story.

---

[26] *Lisa Cron, Wired For Story, Ten Speed Press, 2012.*

Life, of course, isn't lived in slices. It also isn't lived as a series of stories. Or one long novel.

Life tends to just roll along, with no beginning and no end. It's humans that need it to make sense.

Anecdotes, or slices of life, are the everyday events that, out of context, don't mean anything except to ourselves.

A little girl went to visit her grandmother is an event.

A little girl went to visit her grandmother who had turned into a wolf ... is a story starter. We have an immediate, alarming situation here that must change. The change and how it affects granny, little girl, Wolf, their families and the whole shocked community is the story.

We are psychologically set-up to find out what happens next.

Use stories to anchor your main points

We've all seen those list articles – 7 ways to slash your taxes; 5 unique gifts for Dad, 10 ways to save on your next sun vacation...but do you read these and, a week later, still remember all 7 or 5 or 10 of these handy tips? Why would you? Hardly anyone does.

What readers remember are the stories used to jazz those tips. Just part of the power of story is their impact on readers' brains.

Chances are a few weeks from now you won't be able to list all the good writing tips and tools in this book, but I bet you'll recall at least one of the stories I've told illustrating these pointers and the benefits of authoring a book. Stories like these:

Napoleon, age 45, is exiled to one of the dreariest and most remote inhabited places on earth. He's been stripped of everything in life that has meaning for him except a few companions and his own memories. He uses these, despite failing health and other obstacles, to tell his story in the book written to proclaim his legend and assure he overcomes his greatest fear: that he will be forgotten. He dies, imprisoned but not defeated because he has avoided his ultimate hell, oblivion. His book is a success. His legend burns brighter and lives longer than those of any of his enemies.

Former pro athlete Charlie Miller can't win the job and life he wants without performing a task he finds impossible: writing a thesis. A guru/mentor comes to his aid but her plan requires Charlie to trust a young girl he doesn't know to do what he cannot do. Charlie's nerve is tested. If their secret is revealed, he could lose everything. He gambles and wins.

A handsome young man is attracted to a pretty woman, but he just doesn't know what to say to girls. He hires his homely but articulate friend to ghostwrite sweet love letters. It works. Pretty Woman swoons over Handsome Young Man, until she discovers those enchanting letters were written by the best friend, who has long secretly yearned for her love. In this love triangle, which one will she chose? This is the story related in the play *Cyrano de Bergerac*.

Note what is present in these and every story:

1. They start with someone desperately wanting something. This isn't a passing fancy. They want it, need it, must have it. The stakes are high, and they're rising.

2. Doing nothing is not an option.

3. The starting point of the story is the first clash of want meets resistance.

4. Things are going to get worse before they get better (happy ending) or much worse (unhappy ending).

5. At the end, no one is left unchanged.

Stories are always emotional

No emotions, no story. Stories appeal to the heart first; then the mind. Someone will gain, someone could lose. They won't be indifferent and neither will the reader.

Boredom is also an emotion, and it will be the only one you arouse in readers if your book lacks emotional and genuine stories; stories that make people care.

As poet Robert Frost wrote:

"No tears in the writer, no tears in the reader. No surprise in the writer, no surprise in the reader."

If your ghostwritten book does all that I've recommended in this chapter and if the spelling, grammar, punctuation and word choices are correct, your book will demonstrate good non-fiction writing.

Of course, there's more – these are the basics.

The icing on the cake is:

Takeaway

Takeaway from the dinner table is the afterglow. Delicious meal, thoroughly enjoyed with good company.

No indigestion. Just the afterglow.

Takeaway from a non-fiction book is what readers find themselves still thinking about weeks after reading your book. It's also that final, memorable, deeply meaningful sentence or short paragraph that sums up your book.

It can be a quote, a fact, an insight, anything delightful and unexpected. But, once read, so obviously just right.

Before you or your reader can arrive at this happy ending, there may be trouble for you and your ghostwriter that goes way beyond fixing an error, adding another good story or swapping passive for active.

Brace yourself – next we pull on the gloves to tackle these thorns in your book's garden.

You know, everybody has setbacks in their life, and everybody falls short of whatever goals they might set for themselves. That's part of living and coming to terms with who you are as a person.

- Hillary Clinton

NINE | What Could Possibly Go Wrong?

I've written many articles that were, start to finish, like a springtime walk in the park.

Book writing isn't like that.

Writing books, either under my own name or ghostwritten, is never a summer's stroll. There's always something...

There was the book I wrote without a contract. Probably not needed, I thought, because it was for a close friend and the small support group she had started. My friend's group had won a modest grant to produce a book to be given out for free at a clinic for people, like themselves, who'd been diagnosed with one form of cancer. They were trying to reach out and help others.

What they wanted appeared to be straight-forward, a compassionate how-to for people and their families shell-shocked and facing tough choices along with a suddenly uncertain future. The grant money would go to the writer and for printing. My life had also been touched by this illness. I felt I could do justice to the topic, the charity and the readers and write a helpful, useful, gentle and honest book.

Members of the group would serve as both author and editor. After countless revisions, the group finally accepted the manuscript. By now this small charity had become a small registered charity, with a lawyer and a doctor having just joined their board of directors.

The doctor halted the project, until it could be revised, "with proper medical terminology" rather than in the language people with this illness, or their family members, use and understand.

The lawyer declared that the book required disclaimers, more explanation, longer words and less "touchy-feely stuff." The book, she said, would be an official document of the charity proclaiming their contribution to society.

My friend decided, in the face of these objections, that the manuscript could be "more formal."

Soon, not only every board member but every group member, past or present and anyone else they could enlist was going at that manuscript with red pens as sharp as a raptor's claws.

They did this for the next year, passing the bleeding manuscript back and forth. I'm told it led to some lively discussions at their weekly meetings, which I'd stopped attending. I still hoped readers would be helped and comforted by our book, though this was looking less and less likely.

Finally, almost two years after I submitted the final version of the manuscript they'd approved, my friend sent a copy of the finished, very stilted and very slim book.

It was an unrecognizable mish-mash of voice, tone and style – part 'your rights as patient,' part 'how to sound like a doctor when you talk to your doctor,' part heartless lecture about not feeling sorry for yourself and just getting on with life. This book had ice in its veins.

It did not serve readers, did not positively reflect upon the group that had produced it, did not attract more funding and failed as a project.

A lot of things went wrong with that book. They could have been prevented.

1. There was a **lack of clear expectations**. The book I wrote was not, as it turned out, the book they wanted.

2. **Lack of boundaries** – the editing became an almost endless free-for-all. Some members demanded that I refund my part of the grant money (which was much lower than my usual writing fee at the time). I didn't, as the work was as agreed upon and approved (it was the principle of the thing by then).

3. **The needs of readers were forgotten.** A book that is merely a platform for an author's boasting or professional one-up-manship is pointless because it doesn't serve the needs of readers. They will be quick to dismiss a book like this.

4. **Who's the point person?** I took my guidance from the group founder, who simply handed me a pile of research and asked that I use my best judgement to write a helpful, supportive, kind book for readers in crisis. Survivors, not "patients" being condescended to by "experts."

She lost control of the group. Anarchy ensued. Group members inserted blocks of information (and opinion) that weren't part of the initial request and did not align with the book's core message. What a mess!

A successful book (or any other creative work) requires one clear theme, one goal, one mission, one vision, one beating heart, one thinking brain, one caring spirit.

And one cohesive author's voice.

If you do have a group book in mind, elect one person to be the point person and project champion. Decide among yourselves exactly what this book will be, for whom, and why they need it. Then trust your point person as author and ghostwriter as herself or himself to do a good job.

Trust your writer to get it right because, if you can't trust them, why did you engage their writing services?

Some authors think that a pile of papers, a zip file of articles and a few conversations and then the odd email is all a writer will need to complete the book they envision.

Some authors even try to limit the number of conversations and the duration of these conversations in the book contract.

I've seen this happen, with the ghostwriter shackled with an interview limit – so many conversations totalling so many hours. I've never seen a brilliant book come from a shackled writer.

Missing-in-Action authors create a lot of problems. Writers are good communicators, but we aren't mind-readers, able to magically channel the book that lives as a perfect thing in your mind to the page. And we aren't producing widgets stamped from a mould. We need you to make yourself available to answer questions, provide deep insights and to get a true sense of what characterizes your authentic self and voice.

This is your book. You need to be in it all the way, not just as a backseat driver. Or worse, an indifferent passenger.

A ghostwriter friend I'll call Frank struggled with this problem when he took on the writing of a book for a client who had also hired the named author. This is an unusual set up. It came about because the client is a specialty publisher, they wanted this topic on their list and the named author wasn't interested in authorship. He wanted an hourly consulting fee.

The named author would only contribute three hours to the book. Three! In just those three one-hour phone interviews, Frank had to get all the straw to spin into content gold.

Any additional research was up to him, that is, if he could find out anything useful to add. The expert author had a very specific skill area that not a lot had been published about.

Given these limitations, the book is readable, if slight, skating across the topic and generic in voice. The client was satisfied, but as a reader, I was disappointed. The writing is good, but it left me feeling like I'd snacked on the appetizer, then missed the meal.

Poor Frank, stuck with an expert who was shy and barely able to talk to him, while Frank couldn't say "no" to this project because he had to fulfill a pre-existing contract of a certain word count per year to this publisher.

It seemed the unwilling author hadn't ever given what he did, how and why much thought. Not only that, he really didn't care. The interviews with Frank were just another hourly service he'd be invoicing the publisher for.

Believing he had no other option, my friend ended up 'inventing' content, he told me, imagining how a sensible, thoughtful expert might have answered his questions and hoping for the best. The 'voice' of the book sounds just like Frank. The author is the faint shadow.

The publisher accepted the work, Frank accepted his money and, I assume, the author did too and everyone moved on.

Just another forgettable book that short-changed readers.

Gilding the author's lily

I confess, we all do it.

"Nobody," Jane Austen wrote, "minds having what is too good for them."

We writers and journalists make our sources or authors sound good. More organized, articulate, accomplished and successful than they are in life. Smarter. Richer. Bigger. Better looking.

Shinier in every way.

We take out the "ums" and "ahs," the misused words, the clichés, bad jokes, repetition and other clangers and clunkers. While some might not be as noticeable in conversation, they look as weak as they are on the page.

But where do you draw the line between a bit of gilding on a roadside lily and turning that lily into a rose? Or a whole penthouse stuffed floor to ceiling with gilded roses?

As a writer, I know exactly where this line is and so should the ghostwriter you choose.

Perhaps it wasn't quite so clear back in the 1980s for Tony Schwartz when he took on the task of writing **The Art Of The Deal**, Donald Trump's first book.

You can say that Tony Schwartz might have anticipated the problems he'd run into with his author. After all, it wasn't their first time on the boards. Tony Schwartz had already written an unflattering profile of Donald Trump and his wheeling and dealing, one he was astonished to hear Trump was delighted with. [27]

The structure of the book would be simple, Schwartz thought going in. His plan was to tell some stories about Trump's biggest real estate deals, "dispense some bromides about how to succeed in business," [28] and insert Trump's life story. Research would come from a series of conversations. A straight-forward job and a great payday.

But their first session didn't go well. After just a few minutes Trump ushered Schwartz to the door. Successive conversations for the book weren't much different.

Week after week they met, yet Schwartz could get no facts or insights from Trump.

This is a writer's worst nightmare – an author who can't, or won't, contribute to the book's information, insights, quotes and stories.

In desperation, Schwartz called his literary agent to report that the author was stonewalling. After dozens of fruitless attempts, Schwartz was ready to walk away.

But then he rallied. Instead of interviewing the man, he'd change tactics. His new plan was to eavesdrop on Trump's office phone conversations with bankers, brokers, lawyers and

reporters, none of whom would know the ghost was listening and taking notes. Trump agreed.

---

[27] *Jane Mayer, op cit.*

[28] *Ibid.*

For months, Schwartz listened in, crafting the book from what he heard and inventing to fill in the gaps. [29]

In **The Art of the Deal**, "I created a character far more winning than Trump actually is," Schwartz said. What he did, he explained, is write a 'fictional nonfiction' book for his author, with a few setbacks downplayed and many legitimate successes overinflated. [30]

The Art of the Deal, with its cavalier approach to the truth and lack of insights into what makes the real Donald Trump tick, was published in 1989. Trump loved it. His publishers loved it. Readers loved it. It's been a bestseller ever since.

But compare **The Art of the Deal** to a more recent business memoir, **Shoe Dog**, also a hero's journey. The author is Phil Knight, founder, inventor and current Board Chairman of Nike.

Shoe Dog is a warts-and-all telling of one of the world's great brands, ghosted by J. R. Moehringer. It rings with sincerity. We learn the truth about the decades-long rocky path from shaky start-up to world-beating brand.

Bill Gates, heroic leader of another iconic brand, Microsoft, chose **Shoe Dog** as one of his Best Books of 2016, saying "I don't think Knight sets out to teach the reader anything. Instead, he accomplishes something better. He tells his story as honestly as he can. It's an amazing tale!" [31]

---

[29] *Jane Mayer, op cit.*

[30] *Ibid.*

[31] *Bill Gates, op cit.*

Knight doesn't have to boast. He has flaws and regrets and admits them. He shows that he is a success, in part, because he surrounds himself with talented people. The art of his deals lies in attracting top talent and giving them everything they need to excel. He started the ball rolling and kept it rolling on the many occasions when it seemed all was about to be lost. Knight's genius was having the vision and holding onto it, against often daunting odds.

He must have been afraid, often. He didn't gild the lily. He didn't give in or give up.

Fear – the real four-letter F word

Could it be as simple as fear – this compulsive need some people have to appear to be arrayed in gilt while the rest of us are sporting stretch cotton and denim?

Is it fear of strutting out in public like the emperor with no clothes who thought he was luxuriously attired?

Certainly, writing about your thoughts, foibles, insecurities, wins and losses while exposing your deepest feelings and fears for all the world to see, and possibly sneer at, is something like walking around starkers in public.

Out there in the world, we all put on our company face and protective uniform to cover every bruise, bulge, scar and wrinkle. Should we do the same in print?

Should authors do it, with their ghostwriters?

When I think back to my first ghostwritten book, the sociology thesis by the high school gym teacher, I think Fear was a prime factor for my author (or maybe he was just desperately sleep-deprived). A slap-shot lump of pure rubber, travelling at 90 mph (144 kph) directly towards his teeth was something he could live with, and had done for a decade. To him, writing 25,000 or so words about divorce was far more terrifying.

He spoke to me just once. I was armed with what little he said, the *Chicago Style Guide*, his research notes, a chapter outline setting out the then-rigid structure of a thesis dictating what must be in each chapter and the bracing encouragement of Mrs. McCall. Otherwise it was just me, late nights and my powder blue Smith Corona typewriter.

Being 15, I was probably the least afraid of the three of us, believing myself to be bullet-proof, as all teenagers do. So I plunged in. There wasn't time to be overwhelmed, though if I'd had any sense I would have been. And also insisted on a lot more input from the author.

It isn't just novice writers who are prone to overwhelm.

The Peter Pan of Tennis

Even if you aren't a tennis fan, you likely recognize the name: André Agassi. Until his retirement in 2006, he was among the sport's ultra-elite in wins and earnings; at one time voted the best tennis player in the world.

With his wife, Steffi Graff, another tennis legend, he has two healthy children and seemingly a charmed life. Like Donald Trump and Phil Knight, Agassi and his family live near the pinnacle of one-percenters.

André Agassi's book, also written with ghost J. R. Moehringer, reveals a different story. It's another memoir that almost didn't get written, for a very different reason than the Trump book.

In his book, **Open**, André Agassi said he wanted to set the record straight about the many untruths and truths said by him and about him. A powerful and superb tennis player, he also wore earrings, wigs and bizarre outfits on court...took crystal meth and lied about it...set hotel rooms on fire for amusement, and there was more bad behaviour, on court and off. Some would have dismissed his actions as simply the antics of the talented, bored, rich and entitled.

In this book, he said, "I knew I had to expose everything. I think the reader can tell when you're holding back and I also wanted to see my own narrative come into focus. The truth is always surprising." [32]

And not only to readers.

The problem was that no one knew who Agassi was, least of all the man himself.

He was the Peter Pan of tennis.

André Agassi first picked up a tennis racket at age 3, demonstrating real talent when he was 5. From that moment, his life was tennis, tennis, tennis and little else.

His tennis-obsessed father insisted he quit school because it was taking too much time away from practice. Pushed relentlessly, his boy would be a star, a prediction that came true. André became a star and remained a boy. The

---

[32] *Charles McGrath, op cit.*

professional player matured from child to adolescent to man, the skills and reflexes improved. The body matured; the person mostly didn't.

Agassi earned millions in his professional tennis career, reportedly as much as $ 25 million per year during his peak years in endorsements alone. Finally, he chose to retire in 2006 at age 36 when the sport was causing his body to break down and he could no longer beat competitors a decade younger than himself. He has said he hated tennis and always had, but also feared the end of his pro career. He had become a tennis robot. Without tennis, who would he be?

Figuring this out became intertwined with the process of writing **Open**.

"Our first few interviews were just painful," ghostwriter J. R. Moehringer said. [33]

"Stilted, resistant, halting.... he hadn't reached any conclusions about his relationships and couldn't make connections."

J. R. took to reading Freud, Jung, mythology, anything that might help him unlock the locked box of André Agassi. What could he do to get the man to dig deep and talk about what he seemed to know least about: himself?

Both Agassi and J.R. have told Charles McGrath of *The New York Times* that it was tough going. Painful stuff.

Gradually, though, as they kept talking, meeting daily (J. R. had moved to André's hometown so they could have all these conversations in person) things got better. They taped 250

---

[33] *Ibid.*

hours of interviews which were transcribed, boiled down, written, discussed, re-written, polished.

"Some of the book's best passages come almost line for line from the transcripts," J. R. said.

Overcoming overwhelm, together they wrote a compelling book about so much more than one talented athlete's career. It's a moving and true coming-of-age tale.

What Else Can Go Wrong?

Three things:

1. You love the completed manuscript, but your publisher hates it.

Except for literary fiction and poetry, book publishers apply one scale only to anything they plan to publish: will it make money?

If your publisher doesn't like your book, it's because they don't think enough readers will buy your book.

2. You don't like the completed manuscript but your publisher is delighted with it.

Simply because they hear cash registers ringing when they say this.

3. No one likes the completed manuscript except possibly your mum.

Of these three problems, this is the worst. Mums have zero credibility here. Writers try to produce the book you and your publisher (if you have one) will love. I don't have personal experience with this problem, but have heard of it happening. The writer thinks he has done everything his author requested, only to have the book rejected.

Now what? The writer should make the changes you want. If he can't or refuses, one possible choice is to end the relationship and find another writer to fix your book. Or start over.

The way to avoid this or apply damage control is to read, change and approve at every agreed stage of the process, not merely on the full manuscript.

Expect the first version to need changes. First drafts always do. Pros know this.

Books are organic; they grow and change as they are created. They usually become better throughout the process.

Readers won't know or care about the chunks or even entire chapters that had to be re-shaped, re-written, or even chopped from your book.

They are likely to be indifferent to such details as how challenging it was to create this book, how long it took, or what it cost you mentally, physically and emotionally to produce it with your ghostwriter.

All they care about is the benefit to themselves.

I have found that writing a book, like starting a new business, is all about how you solve a series of problems. It is in the solving that your book becomes stronger, self-actualized. It grows up.

NINE | What Could Possibly Go Wrong?

As Phil Knight, father of Nike, says, "When you only see problems, you aren't seeing clearly." [34]

---

[34] *Phil Knight, Shoe Dog, A Memoir By The Creator of Nike, New York: Scribner, 2016.*

The world is what it is; men who are nothing, who allow themselves to become nothing, have no place in it."

- V. S. Naipaul, **A Bend In The River**

TEN | The Power of Becoming an Influencer

You don't need to be a wheeler-dealer casino owner and land developer, a top athlete having an identity crisis, the titan of an iconic product and a blue-chip corporation, current or former royalty, one of the most brilliant military strategists of all time, any flavour of celebrity or the world's best at whatever it is you do to be an Influencer.

An Influencer is simply a thought-leader. Since we all have thoughts and ideas, each of us could potentially lead with those thoughts as Influencer.

Of course, not just any thought will do. Relatively few thoughts are worthy of leadership. Even so, many of these worthy thoughts never are shared, or shared widely enough, to make a difference.

No thought, no matter how worthy, has a hope of becoming influential without a champion for that thought (the brand) and a compelling story involving both the thought and the champion (the brand's big idea in story).

Where's the story?

Journalists are trained to be able to recognize a good story when they see one, even though the story's main players usually can't. Just considering people who've been in the news recently, there are many compelling stories to tell:

- The young girl who live-tweeted events from war-shattered Aleppo after all the journalists had fled.
- The woman who has spent lonely years searching for her sister, who vanished on the Highway of Tears.
- The researcher who has surprising news on the causes of obesity that could change the way we medically manage this problem affecting millions.
- The leader of a group working to save giraffes, recently added to the sad list of the world's endangered animals.
- The scientists who have discovered a shark that can live for 400 years.
- The financial expert who says perhaps young adults shouldn't strive to purchase a home, as their parents did, and what they should do instead to grow financial stability.
- The Japanese professor who is building an android (humanoid robot) that, he says, will soon be able to express emotions. Already, she can carry on an intelligent conversation with people.
- The politician championing tidal power as a new, endlessly renewable source of energy.
- The female CEO of a company in the male-dominated transportation sector who is bringing a fresh take on leadership to an elderly and staid company in challenging times, and winning.

Each of these innovative thinkers could potentially be authors of brilliant, important books that contribute to the national – and even international - dialogue.

...the rest of the story...

If you ever heard Paul Harvey read the news on any of the American Broadcasting Company stations, you'll remember he always ended on a cliff-hanger just before the commercial break, promising to come back soon with "the rest of the story."

Harvey is gone now (he died in 2009) but it's easy to imagine him saying, in his everybody's-favourite-uncle voice, "and now for the rest of the story..."

In the spirit of Paul Harvey, let me tell you what happened next for some of the ghostwritten or co-written books whose stories I've told in this book. Here's how ghostwriters and author-Influencers and their books changed each other and their readers:

1. Charlie Miller – Thesis

Remember the nervous retired athlete who believed his future hinged on what was, for him, the impossible task of writing a thesis? Newly married, he was lumbered with a topic, a literature review of causes of divorce, he hadn't chosen, but his thesis advisor wanted someone to tackle it. Miller drew the short straw. As his ghostwriter, so did I, having never set foot in a college classroom, never taken a sociology course and knowing ziperino about the topic.

I wrote it, the whole time trying to sound like a jock who was writing in an academic style and voice, but somewhat awkwardly. The result had to make readers believe Charlie Miller wrote it.

It did and they did; an audacious battle plan that won the victory.

Charlie Miller finally got his degree and the teaching job at our high school. I got a few hundred dollars to stash in my university savings account. Mrs. McCall got promoted the following year to principal.

Of the three of us – author, ghostwriter, editor -- I think I got the best deal. Unexpectedly, I was presented with an opportunity to learn how to write in an author's voice and style that was very different than my own. The book-length result influenced the readers it targeted, moving them to the desired action. At age 15, I became a successful book ghostwriter.

Not many people get their first career opportunity before they even complete grade 10.

2. Small charity group - Book for people newly diagnosed with cancer

In every way, the book written for the fractious charity group was a failure. Once printed, the group found that they couldn't give it away.

But that's not how this story ends.

My friend, the group's leader, pulled out the version I wrote and submitted it, as the author, to a traditional publisher, with some additional content co-written with a doctor she respected. Though it didn't win any awards, the book did ring up respectable sales (it is now out of print but there are still copies for sale online).

She parlayed her experiences starting that small support group in her living room plus being a published book author into her breakthrough career opportunity and she made the most of it.

Long trapped in a dead-end job, she made the leap to a marketing position with a larger charity and was eventually promoted to director of programming before launching her own company, consulting in the same sector.

I wrote the book, not in one author's voice but in the invented voice of a support group, but that book became hers when she added to it, got a publishing contract and put it to work to achieve her dream job.

3. Donald Trump – The Art Of The Deal

On the June day in 2015 that Donald Trump declared his candidacy for American President, he told a crowd gathered in the lobby of Trump Tower in New York City, "We need a leader that wrote **The Art Of The Deal**." [35]

This, despite partnering on, or working with ghostwriters for several other books in the decades since **The Art Of The Deal** was published in 1987. Clearly Trump sees his first book as the one that declares his world-view, character and personal agenda.

It was this book that extended Trump's reach and influence beyond New York's city limits. When reality-TV producer Mark Burnett read it, he created a new show, *The Apprentice,* with Donald Trump in the spotlight.

Donald Trump made millions in royalties from **The Art Of The Deal**. As influencer, he won the White House.

---

[35] *Jane Mayer, op cit.*

4. Tony Schwartz – The Art Of The Deal

Donald Trump was elated with **The Art Of The Deal** and asked Tony Schwartz to immediately start on another potential bestseller/book-length advertisement for him.

The deal would be lucrative for Schwartz. He already knew his subject. But Trump's first ghostwriter chose to walk away, both from Donald Trump and from ghostwriting.

His journalism career was burnt toast, credibility gone following the Trump book. Instead, he wrote and co-wrote books about business methods and ethics and launched a successful consulting firm that helps companies improve employee productivity by boosting physical, emotional, mental and spiritual morale. [36]

5. André Agassi - Open

André Agassi was already world-famous, with a platform as a winning athlete when he and his ghost worked on his autobiography, **Open**.

The book made him an influencer and thought-leader, but in a very different way than the other ghosted books we've considered.

Tennis made André Agassi and it also nearly destroyed him. He'd earned millions in prize money and endorsements, far beyond enough to qualify for the exclusive American one-percenters' club. But he was broken in body and spirit.

---

[36] *Tony Schwartz author profile on Amazon.com, https://www.amazon.com/Tony-Schwartz/e/B000APMWG0/ref=sr_ntt_srch_lnk_1?qid=14841696 58&sr=8-1*

Reading his book, you get a fascinating behind-the-locker-room-door look at what it's like to be a world-ranked tennis athlete. The more compelling message is what it is to finally find yourself and your true purpose in mid-life.

Open isn't 'just' a sports memoir; it's a coming-of-age story. An awakening, mentally and spiritually.

Today, Agassi doesn't deny his tennis side, but neither is tennis his only side. He and his wife, Steffi Graf, take part in demonstration matches for charity. He runs his own charitable foundation. His charter school for inner city kids is one of its beneficiaries, totally funded by Agassi's foundation. Because of his work, these kids are getting a big chance for better, more meaningful lives than what they go home to every night.

Writing the book, working closely with J. R. Moehringer, helped André Agassi grow into an Influencer changing the lives of others and showing how it can be done.

6. **Napoleon Bonaparte – Memoirs** and **Mémorial de Sainte-Hélène**

Among his other talents, Napoleon was an intuitive marketer. He not only used the media, he controlled it. When he won a great battle, he had paintings made of himself in heroic poses, which were widely distributed and talked about. When he lost, he made sure the French didn't hear about it. Censorship, yes. But also Influence. Thought-leadership. Brilliant brand management. As he said:

"The wise man ignores nothing which helps his destiny." [37]

---

[37] *David McCullough and David Grubin, op cit.*

Napoleon charmed the English captain, officers and crew aboard *Bellerophon*, the ship that took him on the eight-week journey to exile on St Helena. To everyone in Britain at that time, the Napoleon they thought they knew was an ogre, a ruffian, a mad-man. In person, he used his gift to be magnetically charming to win them over.

Once settled in St Helena, Napoleon would exchange letters (heavily censored by his jailers) with British and French sympathisers. The fact that he still had such sympathisers speaks volumes about his personality and character. [38]

He dictated his version of past events and the part he played in them, referring often to maps spread across a pool table, to his friend, Emmanuel, Count Las Casas, an aristocrat who was known as the creator and publisher of an historical atlas. Las Casas was the owner of a mansion in England and had been a soldier in Napoleon's army before becoming an official in his government.

One of Las Casas' qualifications was that he was fluent in English, a language Napoleon (who spoke French and Italian) never learned.

After leaving St Helena in 1816, Las Casas wrote two books: the first taken from his own journal and largely a plea for Napoleon to receive more lenient treatment in exile, published in 1818. It fell on deaf ears.

Napoleon died, most likely of stomach cancer, on St Helena in 1821. Others who shared his exile would write books about that time, some to lasting acclaim. But Count Las Casas'

[38] Brian Unwin, *Terrible Exile: The Last Days of Napoleon on St. Helena*, London: I. B. Tauris, 2010.

Mémorial was published first, in London in 1823. It would be dominant in shaping Napoleon's legacy, just as he had intended.

7. Emmanuel Las Casas - Memoirs and Mémorial de Sainte-Hélène

Las Casas' second book about Napoleon would make him both celebrated and extremely wealthy, earning £ 80,000, [39] which in today's buying power would be more than £ 6.5 million. But rarely has a ghostwriter suffered so much on the path to publication and prosperity.

The close working – and writing – relationship between Napoleon and Las Casas was considered a threat by the Governor of St Helena. He was a bitter man out-ranked and out-flanked by both his prisoners in the past, but now with the thankless (and career suicide) task of being Napoleon's chief jailer.

Governor Hudson Lowe had Emmanuel Las Casas and his ill teenage son, who had accompanied his father to St Helena, forcibly removed from Napoleon's household in chains.

Their trunks were searched and all their possessions including papers seized. Denied medical care, the Count and his son were imprisoned in South Africa.

Repeatedly, the British would seize Las Casas' papers, then return some of them. [40]

---

[39] *Ibid.*

[40] *Peter Friedman, "Emmanuel Augustin Dieudonné: The Real Victor of St. Helena," www.napoleon.org/en/history-of-the-two-empires/articles/emmanuel-augustin-dieudonne-the-real-victor-of-st-helena/*

Finally, the two prisoners were released and they returned to England. On arrival, everything they owned was seized again, they were arrested and sent to Dover, then escorted to the French border, but not allowed back into France. Instead, they went to Frankfurt and then Brussels before quietly slipping back into France.

Las Casas demanded justice from his English persecutors, including the return of all his papers that, under English law, had been seized illegally. This created a huge stir in the English media and debates in the House of Commons in 1818, but only some of Las Casas' papers were ever returned.

As a result, he was forced to write, in part from memory of what Napoleon had told him.

Napoleon died in May of 1821 and was buried on St Helena. But two decades later his remains were brought back to Paris. There, he was given a state funeral in a France now sorely in need of a glorious hero. The younger Count Las Casas – who had been the desperately ill teenager imprisoned with his father – was among those who went to St Helena to bring the remains of Napoleon home.

The map of Europe has been redrawn many times since his death. Unquestionably, Napoleon was arrogant, a tyrant and a dictator responsible for battles and wars in which millions died.

Yet he also created the Napoleonic Code, still the basis of civil law in 70 states and countries, including Louisiana in the United States and the Province of Quebec in Canada. He ended serfdom, established free primary and secondary education for both boys and girls, built libraries, supported the arts and did much more among his liberal reforms.

As British historian Andrew Roberts has written, Napoleon championed and extended "The ideas that underpin our modern world — meritocracy, equality before the law, property rights, religious toleration, modern secular education, sound finances.... a rational and efficient local administration, an end to rural banditry, the encouragement of science and the arts, the abolition of feudalism and the greatest codification of laws since the fall of the Roman Empire." [41]

By any standard, this is Influence.

---

[41] Andrew Roberts, Napoleon: A Life, London: Penguin Books, 2015.

We become what we behold. We shape our tools and then they shape us.

- Marshall McLuhan

ELEVEN | Writing Your Story...What Happens Next?

I hope in this book I have given you the confidence to move ahead in becoming a confident and published book author using the tool of ghostwriting.

No one else has your combination of knowledge, skills and experiences. No one else has what you, uniquely, have to say. Even if you have no time and can't write a book, you now have the strategy, and the information, to become a published author.

Just briefly to recap, this book has told you how to:

- Recognize the benefits of becoming the author of a well-written book.
- Find the best writer to partner with to get your book written.
- Refine your personal brand and describe it in a way that appeals to listeners and achieves buy-in.
- Reveal your Big Idea, the one that supports, enhances and furthers the reach of your personal brand.
- Understand the process of book creation with descriptions of each step.

- Establish and maintain a positive professional working relationship with your ghostwriter.
- Manage your expectations including what it will cost, timelines, goals and what will be delivered to you as author.
- Recognize what your role as author entails; what you contribute to creating an excellent book.
- Understand the publishing process, both traditional and self-publishing, so that you can make an informed choice about which is best for you.
- Recognize quality writing so that you know you have received good value for your ghostwriting investment.
- Reach more readers by actively marketing your book.
- Avoid the possible pitfalls of non-fiction book authorship; with insights into what can go wrong and how to either avoid problems or recover from them.

Become an Author and reap the rewards

Imagine it's a year or so in the future.

You've read this book carefully, perhaps more than once and put its information and advice to good use. Now your book, with your name on the cover, is in your hands.

Your book is better, brighter and delivers even more value to readers than the one you originally set out to create, because you worked closely with a talented ghostwriter.

In the writing, your book has evolved and changed, but not nearly as much as you have. As a published author, your life has changed in surprising ways.

Greater earning power. New opportunities at work. Invitations to speak, join boards of directors or other influential groups. Perhaps a move to another city or part of the world to take up an exciting offer.

A chance to make a bigger bang in the world. And, like Napoleon, not be forgotten.

All because you read this book and put what it says to work to improve your life. You recognized the value of self-promotion through authorship. You took action.

And now you are holding the powerful result. It's a proud moment. Congratulations!

Thanks for reading Get Your Book Written!

Thanks for coming along on this journey into the 'hidden' world of authors and ghostwriters. I hope you found it both intriguing and useful.

As a purchaser of this book, I'd be delighted if you could take just a moment to provide a short review on Amazon.com, Amazon.co.uk or, if you live elsewhere in the world, the Amazon for your country.

I'm passionate about well-crafted books that provide real help and insights to readers, perhaps even changing their lives. While the world certainly has more books than in any earlier era, it is also true that there can never be too many good books. It is this sharing of knowledge along with our fears, dreams and hopes that makes life so much richer and more meaningful.

You can post a review by going to this page on Amazon:

http://amzn.to/2m6AKeD

By reviewing, you help more readers find out about this book – and that could help them in writing their great books to enrich even more readers.

If you have any feedback or questions about the book, I'd love to hear from you. Please contact me via my website.

www.johnsonbookghostwriting.com

Get started on your book!

If you haven't yet, you can download the PDF of the **Get Your Book Written Workbook** with exercises and checklists to accompany the chapters in this book.

http://www.johnsonbookghostwriting.com/GYBW-Bonus/

You'll also receive my infrequent, but helpful emails about writing books and getting them into the hands of readers.

Will I be telling your book creation success story in a future edition of this book? I sincerely hope so! Meanwhile,

Best wishes –

Jacquelyn Elnor Johnson

July, 2017

About the Author

Jacquelyn Elnor Johnson has written more than 20 non-fiction books, both under her own name and as a ghostwriter.

During her three decades as a journalist, she was a reporter, newspaper and magazine editor and publisher. Her hundreds of articles have been published in many magazines and newspapers including *Los Angeles Times*, *Toronto Star*, *Hamilton Spectator* and *Canadian Business*. She has taught writing, journalism and marketing at South Dakota State University and Conestoga College in Ontario.

She holds degrees in English (B.A.), Communications and Journalism (MS) and Business Marketing (MBA). Currently, she is publisher of Crimson Hill Books and is a ghostwriter, specializing in business memoirs and autobiographies, leadership, career development and self-help topics. To discuss a book you want to have written, reach her via **www.johnsonbookghostwriting.com**.

Selected Bibliography

Agassi, Andre, **Open**, Alfred A. Knopf (Random House), 2009.

Bishop, Zealia, "The Curse of Yig," first published in **Weird Tales**, November, 1929.

Carnegie, Dale, **How To Win Friends And Influence People**, Simon & Schuster, Reprint Edition, 2011.

Cialdini, Robert B., **Influence, The Psychology Of Persuasion** (Collins Business Essentials), HarperCollins Publishers, 2009.

Cialdini, Robert B., **Pre-suasion: A Revolutionary Way To Influence And Persuade**, Simon & Schuster, 2016.

Chritton, Susan, "Personal Branding For Dummies Cheat Sheet," from **Personal Branding For Dummies**, 2nd Edition, For Dummies, 2012.

Cron, Lisa, **Wired For Story: The Writer's Guide To Using Brain Science To Hook Readers From The Very First Sentence**, Ten Speed Press, 2012.

Cron, Lisa, **Story Genius: How To Use Brain Science To Go Beyond Outlining And Write A Riveting Novel (Before You Waste Three Years Writing 327 Pages That Go Nowhere)**, Ten Speed Press, 2016.

Dieudonné, Emmanuel Augustus, Comte de Las Casas, **Memoirs of Emmanuel Augustus Dieudonné Count de Las Casas, Communicated by Himself, comprising a letter from Count de Las Casas at St Helena to Lucien Bonaparte, giving a faithful account of the voyage of Napoleon to St Helena, his residence, manner of living, and treatment on that island, also a letter addressed by Count de Las Casas to Lord Bathurst**, London: printed for Henry Colburn, 1818.

Diéudonné, Emmanuel Augustus, Comte de Las Casas, **Mémorial de Ste Hélène, Journal of the Private Life and Conversations of the Emperor Napoleon at Saint Helena By the Count de Las Casas**, London: printed for Henry Colburn, 1823.

Dunninger, Joseph, **Inside The Medium's Cabinet**, New York: David Kemp and Company, 1935.

Fahri, Paul, "Who wrote that political memoir? No, who actually wrote it?" *The Washington Post*, June 9, 2014.

Franks, Sandy, "The Big Idea is Hidden in This 5-Point Checklist," www.awaionline.com/2016/05/the-big-idea-is-hidden-in-this-5-point-checklist/

Franking, Mae M., **My Chinese Marriage**, Duffield, 1921.

Friedman, Peter, "Emmanuel Augustin Diéudonné: The Real Victor of St Helena," www.napoleon.org/en/history-of-the-two-empires/articles/emmanuel-augustin-dieudonne-the-real-victor-of-st-helena/

Gallagher, BJ, "The Ten Awful Truths – and the Ten Wonderful Truths – About Book Publishing," *Huffington Post*, June 5, 2012 and at www.huffingtonpost.com/bj-gallagher/book-publishing_b_1394159.html

Gallo, Carmine, **Talk Like TED: The 9 Public Speaking Secrets Of The World's Top Minds**, St. Martin's Press, 2009.

Gates, Bill, "Best Books of 2016," www.gatesnotes.com

Gladwell, Malcolm, **What The Dog Saw: And Other Adventures**, Little, Brown and Company, 2009.

Gladwell, Malcolm, **Outliers: The Story Of Success**, Little, Brown and Company, 2008.

Goins, Jeff, **The Art Of Work: A Proven Path To Discovering What You Were Meant To Do**, Thomas Nelson and HarperCollins Publishing, 2015.

Halbert, Gary, and Bond Halbert, **The Boron Letters**, Kindle Edition, 2013.

Hebb, Marian D., **The Writers' Union Of Canada: Ghostwriting**, Toronto: The Writer's Union of Canada, undated.

Johnson, Jacquelyn Elnor, **Talk So He Will Listen: 12 Steps To Better Love Relationships For Women**, 2nd Edition, Wolfville, N.S., Canada, Crimson Hill Books, 2016.

Karia, Akash, **Public Speaking: Storytelling Techniques For Electrifying Presentations**, Kindle Edition, 2014, www.amazon.com

Karia, Akash, **How To Open And Close A Ted Talk: 15 Proven Techniques to Open and Close Any Speech or Presentation**, Kindle Edition, 2013, www.amazon.com

King, Stephen, **On Writing: A Memoir Of The Craft**, Hodder Paperbacks, 2012.

Kirkpatrick, David D. "Media Talk; Mrs. Clinton Seeks Ghostwriter for Memoirs," *The New York Times*, January 8, 2001.

Knight, Phil, **Shoe Dog: A Memoir By The Creator Of Nike**, Scribner, 2016.

Kruse, Kevin, "Every Business Professional Needs To Write A Book," *Forbes*, October 3, 2016.

Krznaric, Romain, **Empathy: Why It Matters, And How To Get It**, Tarcher Perigee, Reprint Edition, 2014.

Lamarr, Hedy, **Ecstasy And Me: My Life As A Woman**, Fawcett Crest Books, 1967.

Laming, Scott, "Top 10 Ghostwritten Books," www.abebooks.com/books

LeBlanc, Sydney, "Do You Need a Ghostwriter For Your Book?" *Forbes*, September 5, 2011.

Mayer, Jane, "Donald Trump's Ghostwriter Tells All," *The New Yorker*, July 25, 2016 and at www.newyorker.com/magazine/2016/07/25/donald-trumps-ghostwriter-tells-all

McCullough, David and David Grubin, "*Empires: Napoleon,*" series for television, produced by David Grubin and Allyson Luchak, David Grubin Productions in association with PBS, Docstar and Davillier Donegan Enterprises, 2000.

McGrath, Charles, "A Team, But Watch How You Put It," *The New York Times*, November 11, 2009. Also online at www.nytimes.com/2009/11/12/books/12agassi.html

McKinsey, Dave, **Strategic Storytelling: How To Create Persuasive Business Presentations**, Kindle Edition, www.amazon.com 2014.

McLaughlin, Maurice Evans, **Tennis As I Play It**, George H. Doran, 1915, Kindle Edition republished by Forgotten Books, 2016.

McLuhan, Marshall, **The Medium Is The Massage, An Inventory of Effects**, Bantam Books, 1967.

Norgay, Tenzing, **Man of Everest** [earlier edition titled **Tiger Of The Snows**], G.P. Putman's Sons, 1955.

O`Connor, Maureen, "How To Write Someone Else's Memoir," *New York Magazine*, September 25, 2015 and at www.nymag.com

Ogilvy, David, **Ogilvy On Advertising**, New York: Vintage Books, 1985.

Peterson, Valerie, "Freelance Editorial Costs for Authors," October 18, 2016, https://www.thebalance.com/freelance-editorial-costs-for-authors-2800243

Queen, Ellery, **The Player On The Other Side**, Ellery Queen Mysteries, 1963.

Queen, Ellery, **The Madman Theory**, Ellery Queen Mysteries, republished by Mysterious Press, 2015.

Ray, Pohelia, **Daughter Of The Tejas**, New York Graphic Society, 1965.

Richards, Frank, **Old-Soldier Sahib**, originally published in 1936, republished by Naval & Military Press, 2003, Kindle edition 2015.

Roberts, Andrew, **Napoleon: A Life**, London: Penguin Books, 2015.

Robino, Toni, "Finding Your Perfect Ghost Match," Gotham Ghostwriters Blog, http://gothamghostwriters.com/finding-perfect-ghost-match/

Schachter, Harvey, "Seven Ways Your Lizard Brain Can Improve Your Persuasion Skills," *The Globe And Mail*, November 6, 2016.

Schwartz, Eugene M., **Breakthrough Advertising**, Stamford, CT, United States, Bottom Line Books, 2004.

Shields, Carol and Anne Giardini, **Startle And Illuminate: Carol Shields On Writing**, Random House Canada, 2016.

Strunk, William and E. B. White, **The Elements Of Style**, Pearson, 4th Edition, 1999.

Tamlyn, Sam, "11 Things Your Ghostwriter Doesn't Want You to Know," https://samtamlyn.wordpress.com/articles

Trump, Donald with Tony Schwartz, **The Art Of The Deal**, New York, Random House, 1987.

Unwin, Brian, **Terrible Exile: The Last Days Of Napoleon On St Helena**, London, I.B. Tauris, 2010.

Watson, Jane, **Write On!** Business Writing Basics, Self-Counsel Press, 1996.

Wilson, Arthur, **Lady Malcolm, A Diary Of St Helena 1816-17**, A. D. Innes, 1899.

Zinsser, William, **On Writing Well, 30th Anniversary Edition: An Informal Guide To Writing Non-fiction**, Harper Perennial, 2016.

Acknowledgements

Thank you to the friends who read this book in its early draft and offered valuable feedback, especially Garry White, Carol Zakula and Nancy Tossell.

Also warm thanks to all the members of the Launch Team – thank you so much for your help in getting the word out:

Beverly Adamo, James Archer, Lynne Bard, Valerie Beckett, Michael Blood, Ray Brehm, Hannah Brown, Benjamin Brown, Kristi Burchfield, Julie Carruth, MJR Donis, Jules Fox, Angela Garvin, Sandra Geary, Marty Griffin, Jesse Heaslip, Dave Hegel, Brenda Hewlko, Jay Hildybrant, Jenny Hill, Janet Holmes, Donna Holmes, Kandi Johnson, Jim Molinelli, Marko Pfann, Nancy Priest, Vicky Quigg, Louis Santoro, Nancy Tossell, Wendy Van de Poll, Renee White, Garry White, Dale Wilcox and Carol Zakula.

Special thanks to Dale Wilcox, mentor, inspiration and friend, for writing the Foreword to **Get Your Book Written**. Who knew that way back when I took that part-time writing job, I'd be lucky enough to have Dale as my boss – I've learned so much from her and continue to do so today!

To my home team who are always there to, read, re-read, listen, keep my computer working and do so much more to keep this writer happily at the keyboard, my gratitude and love go to Wayne Johnson and Jesse Bennett Johnson.

And, lastly, thanks to my loyal office assistant, Boots the rescue cat, who keeps me company while I write, rarely interrupts and reminds me of mindfulness, total focus and when it's time for dinner.

- JEJ

www.ingramcontent.com/pod-product-compliance
Lightning Source LLC
Chambersburg PA
CBHW060529210326
41519CB00014B/3179